With much appreciation to my family who is always my biggest fan, my clients whose constant encouragement, trust and loyalty humbles me, my supporters who look forward to my blog posts and books, my Segreto team who continually strive to elevate our craft and inspire me to constantly create, and my design, photography and editing team who put up with my emails at all hours and took my dreams for Segreto Impressions to an entirely different level. Without each of you, I would not have this career that is truly my passion and joy. So, thank you! I am grateful for you all!

————————

BRINGING BEAUTY AND CREATIVITY TO OUR

CLIENTS WITH UNMATCHED CUSTOMER

SERVICE, INTEGRITY, ACCOUNTABILITY AND

ALWAYS A GRATEFUL HEART.

————————

The Segreto Mission

Designer **MARIE FLANIGAN INTERIORS**
Mural **SEGRETO** *Photographer* **JULIE SOEFER**

SEGRETO
IMPRESSIONS

by Leslie Sinclair

IT FEELS LIKE HOME

KITCHENS

Kitchens have evolved into rooms open to living spaces, where guests are entertained and family members gather. Their organization and beautiful design have never been more important in home interiors. Furnish them as a room by dressing the cabinetry with glazes, plastering their hoods, and considering their sheetrock surfaces as you would any other room in your home.

BATHROOMS

Bathroom interiors should bring out your inner beauty, relax your soul, and inspire you to start your day. Their colors should enhance your skin tones, their textures should embrace you, and their lighting should create an ambiance where your best self is reflected when you look into the mirror. What makes you feel soothed, calm, and beautiful? Use these elements to create your own retreat, full of candlelight, bubble baths and a rejuvenated beginning each day.

INNOVATIONS & CREATIVE SOLUTIONS

Architecture and Design **NEWBERRY ARCHITECTURE,**
Builder **GOODCHILD CUSTOM HOMES AND RENOVATIONS,**
Photographer **LAUREY GLENN**

INTRODUCTION

We all want to live beautiful lives and enjoy precious moments in time with those we love. Home is often where we can do that best. It's where we raise our families, entertain friends, and create memories that will carry us through our entire lives.

Not too long ago, I was visiting one of my clients, and she asked her daughter—a young law student—to look through the photographs in my books. After flipping through a few pages, her daughter looked up at me and said, "These are pretty, but what's the point?"

I knew what she was really asking: How does what you do make the world a better place? I thought, *fair question.*

"For me, having the opportunity to visually translate my clients' inner beauty into their interiors is deeply rewarding," I said, "because it gives them a feeling of contentment and happiness at home. This warm feeling, in turn, translates positively into many aspects of their lives."

She looked around the picturesque home where she grew up, smiled, and said, "Can I be a part of the process?"

After that moment, I went on to do a lot of soul-searching into why I'm so passionate about creating beauty in people's lives. In many ways, this book is what I discovered through that search.

So let's go on a journey together: one of living more beautifully at home. The interiors will be our muse; the homeowners, our guides; and the trades who collaborated to bring these visions to life, our coaches.

There are so many tiny, everyday experiences that make up our lives—drinking coffee from a special mug or setting the table for a family gathering—and each moment deserves to be cherished. It's my humble hope that this book empowers you to craft a home that reflects your inner self and helps you discover who you really are or aspire to be.

LESLIE

IT FEELS
LIKE HOME

Homes should be a reflection
of our inner selves: places
where we feel safe, where we
rejuvenate and share meaningful
time with family and friends.

PARISIAN APARTMENT

DESIGNER MEG LONERGAN
ARCHITECT TOM WILSON & ASSOCIATES
RENOVATOR PINTAIL CONSTRUCTION
PHOTOGRAPHER PÄR BENGTSSON

This 1930s home is located in a beautiful historic district where graceful oaks line the street. After falling in love with the neighborhood, lot size, and layout of the house, the new homeowners found themselves perplexed about how to integrate their chic modern art and furnishings into a more classical interior. Designer Meg Lonergan had worked with the couple on past projects and was brought on board to reinvent the interiors to blend with the clients' design aesthetic. The concept of "Parisian Apartment" was born.

The exterior was left virtually untouched while the interiors began to reflect the youthful, vibrant personalities of the homeowners. Paneling was simplified for a cleaner look while the intricate crown moldings were preserved and painted in a high-gloss warm white, giving a sleek perspective to their European-inspired carvings. The starting color inspiration? A wool fabric that would be used to drape the windows throughout the home. Segreto was brought in to translate the color into a plaster that would complement the glow of the paint sheen while creating a soft backdrop for the contemporary art and eclectic furnishings. I was excited to be a part of the project, especially since I already had a connection to this home: I worked with the previous owner on their vision of the same space. Many things changed to fit the new owner's style but this ceiling, which we finished to feel reclaimed, looked beautiful in both design interpretations.

Music is a passion for these homeowners, and the sound systems are as important as the luxurious silk, velvet, mohair, and wool fabrics that infuse the modern furniture with such deep comfort. In the formal living, plaster shelving was installed to hold equipment in a clean, chic way. Full of youth, fun, and excitement, the clients embraced bold choices like the International Klein Blue Venetian plaster bathroom, a German Eggersmann kitchen, and a high-gloss ceiling in the formal living.

International Klein Blue
is a deep blue hue first
mixed by the French artist
Yves Klein in the late '50s.
Developing it to use in his
monochrome paintings, he
felt the color alone evoked
a boundless vision. Working
with a chemist to add
the pigment to a binding
medium, he patented the
product as IKB and began
using this color almost
exclusively. I discovered
how hard this exceptional
color is to emulate—it took
us many versions to get it
right. Ultimately, it worked
beautifully in Venetian
plaster, a rich plaster with
a high, marble-like sheen
made from a fine lime putty
and marble dust.

The dining room ceiling was plastered in a barely mint tone, then waxed. The drapes in this room were made from the same wool used throughout the home, but here they were lined with fabric of the same color—a detail that Meg loves!

Most people who visit the home are wowed by the media room's paneled detail and color. Starting with Farrow & Ball Green Smoke for the paneling, we customized a waxed plaster to blend. Perfecting this color was challenging but well worth the effort.

The addition of the modern kitchen changed the entire feel of the house. The simplicity of the plaster that rolls onto the hood complements the sleek lines of the Eggersmann kitchen. These kitchens are distinguished both by unique fronts and technological advances that are individualized for each homeowner.

The master suite's plaster tone is imbued with a whisper of the drapery color. Comfortable and modern, the consistency of the trim color and unlacquered brass rods used throughout provide a natural flow with the rest of the home.

Her master bath was updated using the existing tile and marble and incorporating modern fixtures and new lacquered cabinetry painted in Benjamin Moore Seattle Mist. His bath took a masculine turn with use of warm natural stones and brass fixtures. The remaining surfaces were plastered, becoming the connecting factor throughout.

MODERN FRENCH

DESIGNER MoL DESIGN

ARCHITECT CHARLES W. LIGON AIA ARCHITECTS INC.

BUILDER KRISTAL CONSTRUCTION

PHOTOGRAPHER WADE BLISSARD

The first time I met Ashley, she was sitting across from me asking to work for Segreto for free. Passionate about antiques, Ashley was mesmerized by how finishing could transform pieces. She was an avid Segreto follower, reading our blog and studying our design books. Inspired by her passion and willingness to learn, I hired her on the spot—paid, of course—with no idea if she had a good color sense, except for the fact that her makeup was perfectly applied, complementing her eyes and skin tone.

After Ashley left Segreto to start an adventure of her own—Renouveau, an antique import company—we stayed in touch. Years later, Ashley and her husband decided to build, and we once again found ourselves sitting across from each other at that same table, this time talking about what she envisioned for her new home. Her love of Europe and 18th-century antiques was her inspiration. Creating peaceful, comfortable spaces with the natural, effortless feel of French design was her aspiration.

Ashley hired designer James Mol, who balanced her over-the-top tendencies with his own minimalistic design style, and the adventure began. Taking buying trips together, they returned with European treasures: 15th-century beams from the Couvent des Jacobins in Toulouse, reclaimed limestone floors and 18th-century light fixtures. Under Ashley and James' artful eyes, many antiques were revitalized with fresh purpose, such as the 16th-century mantel used for the kitchen hood, French street lamps converted to pendant lighting, and the Italian console, customized with a SegretoStone® integrated sink that became the powder bath basin.

Plaster radiates and reflects light in the entry ceiling, soaring over antique pieces including an artisan-crafted console from France and a mirror flanked with 17th-century angels from an Italian cathedral. The simplicity of the wrought iron railings dying into the plastered walls, while tedious to implement, creates a dramatic impact set against the beauty of the home's minimalist architecture.

For James, the starting point was the home's architecture. He removed details from the plans that he felt would dilute the home's beauty, ensuring the bones felt authentic and clean. The furnishings incorporate antiques mixed with clean-lined, classical modern upholstered pieces.

Ashley and James were determined to have the spaces be uncontrived, and the finishes played a huge role in creating that essential authenticity. The white plaster gives a softness to the walls that merges naturally with the reclaimed elements of the home while infusing a sense of modernism. The uncoated trim and walls were painted to blend in Sherwin Williams Zurich White.

The 18th-century surround for the bar was purchased before the architectural plans were drawn. When building with reclaimed elements, it's ideal to know the dimensions during framing as retrofitting to work in the space can be expensive. The SegretoStone® counter with integrated sink adds a beautiful visual to the space without detracting from the uniqueness of the antique feature.

The counters deepen the organic feel for the home and were a last-minute design addition. Ashley and James arrived at Segreto armed with their selected marbles for a final color consult, where they spied our new signature line of plaster countertops and sinks. Instantly, the duo felt strongly they were the only "right" choice for their surfaces, and we chose a white polished finish to blend naturally with the tones of the walls.

SegretoStone® countertops line the kitchen, which is the heart of the house. Says Ashley, "The countertops with the integrated sinks put the house over the top for me." A 16th-century mantel hovers over the stovetop, the 18th-century doors under the sink are from a French farmhouse, and the fixtures over the island were once streetlights in France.

The home would not even be close to our vision without the plaster. Our furnishings and architectural elements are illuminated with the luster of the walls. They are authentic and quiet, yet romantic, and so peaceful.

ASHLEY, HOMEOWNER

*Tranquility reigns in the master
bath, where we used a waterproof
Tadelakt plaster in the shower and
SegretoStone® countertops with
integrated sinks.*

CLASSIC MODERN

DESIGNER SLOVACK-BASS
BUILDER CK&H CONSTRUCTION

Margie Slovack has worked with this family of seven on half a dozen major projects over the course of twenty years, as their family has grown and their needs changed. When the family purchased their latest home, it had a stark interior highly specific to the previous owners. To turn it into the collected yet modern home the family wanted, the design team started with a room-by-room walk through, taking the needs of each family member into consideration—even their dog, Benji. The goal was to imagine how the family would live and move through their new home. From this early vision, the background palette was chosen, which provided the basis for all the hard surface, fabric, and furnishing selections. Together, homeowners and design team envisioned a balance of clean and simple background elements and spectacular wall textures. After their thorough review, they decided to replace the downstairs flooring, reposition the entry next to the study, create a club room with a striking bar backdrop, and float the dining table between the kitchen and gathering room.

The textured, layered walls are truly the star of this space, countered with the moody sheers and modern touches that take a moment to absorb.

MARGIE SLOVACK, DESIGNER

The entry and adjacent study were re-imagined to spark curiosity, using layers of color and texture in contrasting hues. A multi-toned Venetian plaster serves as a backdrop for the stunning, mirrored storage cabinet, elegant writing desk, and ample seating. Adorned with artwork that reflects the homeowner's history of collecting pieces that speak to her, the space is both glamorous and friendly.

Positioned between the elegant entry and dining space, the bar in the club room was restructured, incorporating new slab-front panels and waterfall drops. Custom club chairs and an acrylic-legged ottoman sit under a cloud-like ceiling, creating a cosmopolitan feel and a place for visitors to relax and join the conversation. This room is completely open to the gathering room—a spacious, two-story, light-filled arena set up for family activity.

I was excited to see this painting by Kiah Denson from The Segreto Gallery, which was purchased for their previous home, look so beautiful in this home's new interpretation.

New cabinet doors finished with a grained whitewash transformed the mood of the kitchen. They are framed with the original dark cabinetry with new backsplash materials of mosaic and tinted, bronzed mirror.

This busy kitchen is home to a serious cook, and it has the perfect combination of action spots and seating for ten. To avoid the expense of rebuilding the kitchen and replacing the counters, they instead made a few tweaks. The back-painted glass top seems to float on the new veined flooring in this dual-use space.

CONTEMPORARY OASIS

DESIGNER TRISHA MCGAW DESIGNS
BUILDING DESIGNER ROBERT DAME DESIGNS
BUILDER ALLAN EDWARDS BUILDER INC.
PHOTOGRAPHERS JULIE SOEFER, WADE BLISSARD

Seeking to create a tranquil retreat for their family located close to downtown, this couple discovered a home in framing stage, tucked away on a spacious lot. They immediately could visualize the exterior settings with water features and landscapes reminiscent of Cabo San Lucas. This seaside resort city is a place close to their hearts, one filled with fond family memories; a place where they'd felt both deeply relaxed and inspired by the natural rock-and-azure beauty. They wanted to create these feelings and evoke these cherished memories in their home. Their struggle came in determining whether the interiors of this extravagant Mediterranean dwelling could be reinterpreted to reflect their contemporary style. They found their leap of faith in the confidence they felt with Trisha McGaw and Allan Edwards, the same design and build teams who had worked with them on their previous house. Together, they embarked on a journey to transform this classic European into their own unique contemporary resort.

The interiors of this house embody the unexpected. As you open the door, you assume a Mediterranean décor is ahead. Instead, you're ushered into a fresh, contemporary aesthetic. The graceful curved walls, columns, two-story rooms, and balcony-style hallways infuse the spaces with interest. The sweeping curvature of the architecture brings your eyes to the outdoors and creates the feeling of an open-air retreat, working in harmony with the exterior landscape to conjure a sense of one large entertaining space. From every room in the house, the outdoors becomes part of the interior through large expanses of floor-to-ceiling windows and balconies furnished like rooms.

Finishes play a large role in making the expansive space feel inviting. The refined white plaster hugs the dramatic architecture, creating a soft sheen and contemporary ambiance to what could have felt old world if painted in a dark tone or coated in a rustic material. The white textured finish of the columns, with touches of warm browns peeking through, balances the sleekness of the walls and lends an established feel to the home. These foundations, mixed with the organic feel of reclaimed woods, SegretoStone® plaster countertops and feature walls, and contemporary custom lighting, set the tone for the contemporary art and custom transitional furnishings.

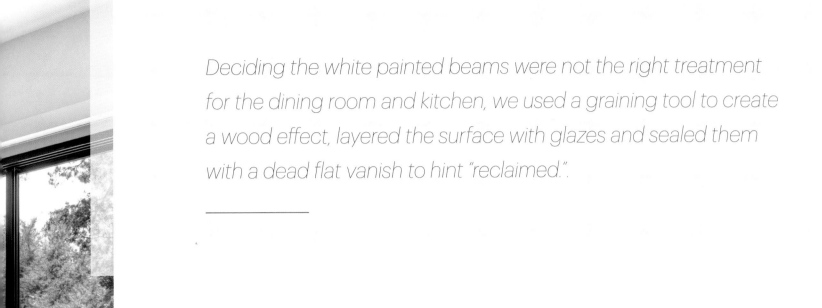

Deciding the white painted beams were not the right treatment for the dining room and kitchen, we used a graining tool to create a wood effect, layered the surface with glazes and sealed them with a dead flat vanish to hint "reclaimed.".

Large in scale, the slated family room became the current dining room. With ample room to house a custom designed 12-foot by 5-foot table, the new space invites welcomed guests to dine comfortably while taking in the incredible views.

A SegretoStone® counter acts as a bridge, blending organically with the reclaimed wood bar top and rich silk wallcovering.

The master suite is a retreat of its own. The infusion of warm woods and white plaster showcases the open fireplace wall dividing the sitting and sleeping spaces. The closet's cabinetry, adorned with mirrored door fronts and contemporary crystal lighting, gained a subtle metallic effect. By glazing and brushing a sealer infused with metallic powder on top of the woodwork, we mimicked the shimmer of a fine silk. The five-star spa feel of the bath marries perfectly with bedroom furnishings that hint at the Hollywood era, creating an intense feeling of comfort you can only experience at home.

The redesign of the master closet was one of Trisha's greatest challenges. Framed with curved walls, she redrew the spaces to be square to maximize every bit of wall space. The closet's footprint actually was reduced in size, however twice as much room was created to house shoes, purses and clothes. With mirrored fronts, metallic finished cabinetry and jeweled hardware, this space has an opulence all its own.

IT'S ALL IN THE MIX

DESIGNER AMY MURCHISON
RENOVATOR URBANCRAFT CUSTOM BUILDERS, LP
PHOTOGRAPHER WADE BLISSARD

After living in this home for more than 10 years, these empty nesters with a gaggle of grandkids and two giant Labrador Retrievers, Oliver and Mitch, decided an open floorplan would better fit their lifestyle. They both love rock-and-roll music, and he has an incredible guitar collection and plays multiple instruments. Wanting the interiors to make them feel happy and energized like their music does, the homeowners hired Amy Murchison to transform this very traditional home into one filled with color, a sense of flow, and a lot of light.

Taking down walls to open up the spaces to one another and installing large metal doors and windows flooded the rooms with sunshine. The new color palette was inspired by the Ashley Longshore painting of Audrey Hepburn that was purchased for the living room. All the colors were selected from the florals in Audrey's headpiece, from the yellow silk drapery that gives continuity to the multiple seating areas, to the pillows made from Casamance fabric, to the accessories and upholstered pieces.

Amy sought balance for the vibrant use of color through her choice of wall treatment, neutral floors, and the introduction of a sleek black mantel. A bright white plaster was infused with a hint of yellow ochre for a subtle warm glow, applied to all the walls throughout, and then waxed. This provided a beautiful backdrop to the carefully curated art, and the sheen allowed the light to bounce off of the polished walls. The trim and ceilings were painted Farrow & Ball Pointing to blend.

The homeowner felt strongly about keeping the mirror in the dining room. We gave it new life by embellishing with gold leaf and tweaking the color to better work with the Jim Thompson fabric of the console table.

Amy has parlayed her eclectic fashion sense into her design philosophies. For the most part, practical comfort is at the forefront—but sometimes it's the splurge on those totally over-the-top gorgeous heels that completes the look. At first, the homeowners wanted all new, modern furniture. Ultimately, they embraced Amy's vision of incorporating a few antiques for juxtaposition and a distinctly fresh, contemporary interior. The entry chandelier from Winston Contemporary Art combines both vintage and modern. This culmination of scavenged old objects is recreated in a modern light by artist Andy Coolquitt and makes a playful statement of what's to come as you enter the home. As Amy says, "It's all in the mix!"

SERENITY IN TRANSITION

DESIGNER JJ DESIGNS

BUILDING DESIGNER RICE RESIDENTIAL DESIGN, L.L.C.

BUILDER GOODCHILD CUSTOM HOMES AND RENOVATIONS

PHOTOGRAPHER WADE BLISSARD

This traditional brick home was built by the family's in-laws 30 years ago, and it's filled with cherished memories of raising a family and entertaining friends. As they saw their needs changing, the homeowners made a decision: they wanted to redesign their existing home by creating more functional open spaces, without enlarging the footprint. They imagined a larger kitchen, more space in the den for their family to gather, an outdoor entertaining area, a roomy master bath and closet, and a light, open, updated feel throughout the home. Their imaginative drive spurred them to assemble a team that would work creatively together to bring their visions to life.

The natural finishes make a major contribution to the warmth one feels when entering the home. The reflective quality of the plaster glows as you move throughout and gives a new sense of height to lower ceilings. Wall finishes, glazed cabinetry, Belgian bluestone, consistent use of wood through the main areas, and natural marbles and quartzes create a beautiful backdrop for the layered fabrics, thoughtfully purchased antiques, comfortable furnishings and well-placed accessories. This new look revitalized the bones of this legacy home and the lives of the sweet family who live here.

Adding footage to the front porch, finishing the new front doors and shutters in a warm, textured application, and painting the existing red brick added fresh curb appeal to what had been a traditional façade.

JJ Designs set the new tone of the home, moving away from the golds and reds that had defined spaces to a lighter, brighter overall palette infused with the homeowners' favorite soothing blues. This opened up the spaces visually, creating an airy, ethereal flow. With preliminary plans drawn, the renovation began. The kitchen was enlarged by taking in part of the living room, which allowed for repositioning the angled island, building an appliance tower, and adding a dry pantry for extra storage. Newfound room for cabinetry meant an extra window could be added to frame a beautifully tiled feature wall with open shelves and a plastered hood. The cabinetry was enhanced with a dry brushing and edging technique, which lends interest to this French-style kitchen without darkening the surface or creating a distressed look.

The windows were replaced with larger panes for more uniformity. Widened casements throughout the home lend a more open feel and encourage people to move easily from room to room during parties and get-togethers.

Initially, when we were selecting finishes, my husband was unsure about the plaster. He saw the subtle variation as inconsistencies in the treatment. After it all came together, he loves how it adds such a warm and inviting feel to our home, and he's thrilled about its durability and easy care! Recommendation: take your husband to show him the finished product before you start the process!

HOMEOWNER

By keeping wall, ceiling, and trim color consistent, a home with traditional moldings and style will feel more open and take on a transitional style. To complement the plaster color, Benjamin Moore Vanilla Milkshake was selected as the trim color.

To enhance the richness of the polished nickel hardware in the master, we added a silver leafing to the bead detail of the door fronts. This provided an enticing bit of glamour to the glazed cabinetry. I can't say strongly enough how important it is to meet with your finisher before construction begins. Our preliminary meetings helped to ensure the style of the cabinetry would translate well with the right finish for this space.

The master suite has become a refuge, incorporating soothing blue-gray plaster tones, floor-to-ceiling sheers, and cozy seating for a morning cup of coffee or a good book. The bath took its color inspiration from the marble floors, counters, and inset mosaic in the shower. The plaster and softly glazed cabinets married all these elements, while the mirrors expanded the space.

SPANISH REVIVAL

ARCHITECTURAL CONSULTANT AND DESIGNER
SARAH WEST & ASSOCIATES
RENOVATOR PARKER HOUSE, INC.
PHOTOGRAPHER PÄR BENGTSSON

When I walked into the office for a new client meeting, I had no idea it would be with an old friend from high school. She wasn't expecting to see me either. (I use my married name, and, truth be told, most people think I am Leslie Segreto). We dove into catching up on our lives and discussing her newly purchased Mediterranean home. I discovered she was a photographer, horseback rider, animal lover, and art collector with an appreciation for Native American artifacts. Her vision was for a Spanish-style home, filled with reclaimed elements, that felt warm and inviting and reflected her lifestyle and passions. We looked at different plasters, worn woods, and SegretoStone® counters and scheduled a walk through of her new home. After seeing its traditional architecture, I suggested she hire Architectural Consultant Sarah West to bring her vision of a warm Spanish revival to life.

Embracing the homeowners' love of history, Sarah wanted this home to tell a story. Through the large steel doors veiled in antique shutters created from a family barn, the entry is filled with carefully curated art that is anchored by the warmth of antique floors and rugs. Stone was added to archways, the new wrought-iron staircase railings were given an aged patina, and the walls and ceilings were wrapped in a warm, reflective white plaster, all giving shape and depth to the home's emerging Hacienda style.

The library was transformed into an artful display of the owner's collection of Native American artifacts. We constructed shelves from our new SegretoStone® product and cantilevered them off the walls, providing an interesting floating base for this incredible grouping. Sarah centered vintage airplane chairs upholstered in golden suede around a period brass and glass coffee table, creating a cozy seating area to visit and enjoy the art.

Designed with the cook in mind, the kitchen and keeping room are spaces that encourage gatherings filled with warm conversation. The Spanish-style plastered fireplace, beautiful terra-cotta and reclaimed wood ceiling, waterfall island, and SegretoStone® hood all blend the warmth of the past with today's luxury. Sarah, who often encourages clients to mix various periods of furniture, here incorporates mid-century modern velvet chairs with an antique Spanish breakfast room table.

The glisten of the focal, antiqued, mirrored wall and vintage Murano glass lighting balances the antique sink, door, and tile floors. Plaster becomes the perfect backdrop for rooms that incorporate statement pieces like these.

For me, texture is one of the most important elements in creating a well-used powder room. In this space, I immediately knew we could create a sense of importance by cladding the walls with a horizontal-textured wood and having Segreto apply a specialty plastered and waxed finish. We continued the treatment down the mudroom and entry hall and into the powder room where it wraps around the base of a custom-designed SegretoStone® sink.

SARAH WEST, DESIGNER

The master suite evokes the feel of both romanticism and comfort with its use of soft fabrics and shades of blue that complement the art of the American West. The fireplace wall hosts a vintage panel of antique tile, anchored by plastered benches. The inspiration for the bath was the most beautiful antique Parefeuille ceiling tile, installed as flooring.

These tiles were a wonderful find of Sarah's, and a story all their own. They were uncovered from within a painted ceiling, where parts had been shielded from paint by beams. The reclaimed tile was used as flooring with the remainder cut into smaller pieces and installed in the tub vestibule to create a wonderful focal wall. We applied a thinned-down plaster in the same tone of the plastered walls, to soften its look and offset the wall tile from the floor.

The rich color in the master closet was the perfect palette to host the owner's collection of cowboy boots. Vintage Hermès scarves framed in brass add a visual layer that connects to the antique rugs and collection of boots and hats. The rich color of the room couples with layered Spanish rugs, brass hardware, and lighting for a casual yet chic retreat.

CALMING RETREAT

DESIGNER THE OWEN GROUP DESIGN FIRM
ARCHITECT ARCHITECTURAL SOLUTIONS, INC.
BUILDER LISENBY CO INC
PHOTOGRAPHER WADE BLISSARD

Hired by builder John Lisenby to give his high-end spec home the feeling and personality that would inspire someone to purchase, designer Tami Owen and her team were brought in early on. Starting with a set of plans, Tami's brain began to turn. She wanted every room to feel special—peaceful, elegant, and timeless. And she was in search of a handful of really remarkable, stand-out elements that would make prospective buyers take notice.

Working with architect Travis Mattingly, the team decided to keep the trim to a minimum and allow the plaster incorporated throughout the home to enhance the architecture's clean lines. To achieve a consistent palette, a white plaster was selected, and the trim was painted Benjamin Moore White Dove to blend. The spacious entry hall has expansive openings that lead to different rooms, creating a wonderful flow for entertaining.

Tami envisioned a new use for a front room that was slated to be a study. "Studies at the front of the house are rarely used and often cluttered," she said. Her idea? Turn the space into a cocktail room to expand the entertaining landscape. Steel doors open up to a veranda-like garden complete with a fire pit, becoming an extension of the room when entertaining or a special place to enjoying the evening with a good glass of wine.

The velvet texture of the plaster walls sets the tone for the eclectic mix of furnishings.

TAMI OWEN, DESIGNER

As the home was nearing completion, Tami discovered dear clients of hers were looking to move. She showed them the project, and they felt a connection at first glance. From that point on, Tami was able to furnish the home to fit this family's kid- and pet-friendly lifestyle, love of casual gatherings, and philanthropic entertaining.

The kitchen incorporates a wood Versailles pattern island counter, metal hood, Calacatta marble slabs, and top-of-the-line appliances.

SPANISH COLONIAL

DESIGNER GARRETT HUNTER

ARCHITECT MICHAEL LANDRUM

BUILDER MORRIS HULLINGER

PHOTOGRAPHER PÄR BENGTSSON

The frequent team of architect Michael Landrum and designer Garrett Hunter always inspires me when we collaborate on projects. I think it's because I never know what to expect. No two homes I have worked on with this duo have been even remotely similar. This contemporary take on Spanish colonial is no exception. Wanting an airy and time-transcending style to complement the collected look that Landrum and Hunter are known for, we selected a mottled plaster with depth in color for the home. Hugging the clean lines of the architecture and the sculptural presence of the impressive staircase, this finish offers a cohesive element and sets the mood for the home's eclectic interior furnishings and art.

Garrett is a master editor of furniture and objects; each is given breathing room to tell a story of its own. Curating and personally sourcing each piece, he incorporates unique items such as the striking Olivier Gregoire Fold series fiberglass chair designed for the fashion label Acne, the Ginkgo chair from Garrett and Michael's own Tienda X furniture line, and the Charles James sofa. It's an ethereal, relaxing, utterly original space.

Design has the unspoken power to change moods, to make life easier. The mark of good design is beyond the eye, and all about how it makes you feel. Sometimes the best details are the details that you don't even notice.

GARRETT HUNTER
DESIGNER

The chic, beautifully designed kitchen took quite the team effort to realize. The floating hood in front of the steel window rolls seamlessly into the ceiling. Before it was installed, the hood was first plastered on all sides. Later, it was fastened to the ceiling, allowing us to plaster the rest of the space and blend the seams so they were undetectable. Difficult? Yes, but well worth the effort. The refrigerator panels—art pieces commissioned from Jaime Loera—created a furnished room feel, crucial for a kitchen that sits within an open floor plan.

No detail escapes thought and attention. Grillwork at the front door allows for more privacy while flooding the space with light. Michael's inset lighting features, contemporary take on the iron wine cellar doors, floating fireplace wall, and spacious hallways are all creative and unexpected solutions that enhance the client's experience of living within their home.

The finishes in this particular project react to one another in especially interesting ways. As designer Garrett Hunter said to me, "They're like a great film! The leading actors have the big moments, but the supporting actors are just as important."

COUNTRY FRENCH

DESIGNER LUCAS/EILERS DESIGN ASSOCIATES L.L.P.
ARCHITECT ARCHITECTURAL SOLUTIONS, INC.
BUILDER ABERCROMBIE CUSTOM HOMES, L.P.
PHOTOGRAPHERS WADE BLISSARD, JULIE SOEFER

This home was exciting for me to see unfold. Tempted at the prospect of less maintenance and the ability to lock and leave, my husband John and I considered downsizing and building on a smaller lot in a nearby neighborhood. Purchasing a plot in one of Abercrombie's developments, we decided to build. Cold feet set in, with a shared sense that the timing of this move wasn't right for us, and we sold the lot back. Much to my thrill, Sarah Eilers called me in to collaborate with the couple who were building on that very same spot!

Kathy and Doug harbored similar reservations to our own. Going from a half-acre with beautiful trees to a small lot that backed up to another house was a concern for them. Would they feel too confined, or too close to the house next door?

They wanted a home that was comfortable, relaxing and not fussy. They hoped to incorporate some of their special family heirlooms into the décor, along with a few pieces of modern art. Knowing they would spend most of their time in the kitchen and living areas, architect Travis Mattingly created views to the outside of a small patio and yard, lending an open and spacious feel. Landscape architect Lee Klopfer created a charming courtyard that features an antique French fountain. When the steel doors to the living room are left open, the garden shares its soothing waterfall sounds. The walls and ceilings throughout the home were plastered, enhancing its architecture and heightening that relaxing feeling from the moment you walk through the front door.

One of the project's greatest challenges? The homeowners didn't want a visible TV in the living room. Nor did they want to look into the living room and think, "Oh, there's a TV hidden behind those panels." How could the television be made invisible? After a lot of research, they discovered an "art lift" that would completely mask the television. Making it work would require some precise planning and engineering, from the size of the art piece to the indentation in the wall that would house the lift. Thanks to many consultations with designer and builder, as well as a fine art framer who worked to exact measurements, the lift works perfectly. It even has the ability to function with the push of a button on their iPhones.

The doors leading to the study fold back and inset into a vestibule wall, framing its entrance like panels when left open. Constructed from paint-grade wood, they were finished to feel stained, highlighting their crevasses to accentuate their beautiful shape.

*The traditional furnishings
and contemporary art form
a beautiful environment for
a blend of materials and
textures throughout the home.*

SARAH EILERS
DESIGNER

Sarah was invaluable in helping mix old and new in a tasteful manner. Her steady hand and expert eye eased the homeowners' concerns about avoiding the look of a mish-mash of different styles, and creating a true marriage of old and new. Sarah blended antique furnishings and contemporary comforts, along with special family heirlooms, to create a light and airy respite. Due to the open floor plan, a soft taupe plaster was used throughout with the exception of the study and master retreat, which each received a personality all their own. The kitchen cabinets were given a finish we created with a bit of sand, lending a quiet patina and complementing the reclaimed oak floors and beams. With the backsplash left to last, the perfect antique cement tile was discovered on a shopping trip to Chateau Domingue and pulled everything together. The stone hood, colorful tiles over the stove, and lanterns above the island add interest to the space. Painting the white vents, speakers and rims around the canned lighting to blend with the reclaimed wood on the ceiling was the finishing touch in this beautiful space.

The master retreat is composed of a spacious bedroom, sitting room, coffee bar, and a luxurious master bath. The main house plaster tone flows into the master sitting room. Wanting a different feel for the bedroom and bath, these walls were plastered in gradations of the most relaxing shade. I call the color Blaygeen, which is inspired by the wonderful French interpretations of blue, mixed with subtleties of green, gray and umber. Their new space is the realization of their desire for a home that is comfortably elegant in the spirit of the French countryside.

The design for the master bathroom started with the quartzite slabs for the countertops and shower. The white and gray color palette paired well with the adjoining master sitting room and its blue hues. Some of the details that elevate this space include mosaic tiles on the floor that look similar to a rug, three antique mirrors, and the multi-leveled countertop that creates a functional vanity.

CLASSIC EUROPEAN

DESIGNER OHARA DAVIES-GAETANO INTERIORS
PHOTOGRAPHER WADE BLISSARD

Today's interior trends are moving away from overstated Mediterranean, heavy in architecture, dark paneling, and faux textures, to cleaner, classic European design. Homeowner Laureen had worked with California-based designer Ohara Davies-Gaetano on her West Coast beach house and knew she was the perfect fit to revive their primary residence in Houston. First simplifying some features, Ohara ultimately infused the house with a new, softer, timeless palette, shedding heavier tones and finishes and stripping down overdone interior architectural details that felt contrived. She added antique architectural pieces to create a sense of history and soul in this newer home.

The home's layout, built around a beautiful pool in the center and golf course view to the back, had a wonderful flow. As she started the design process, Ohara saw an opportunity to transform the long hallway that runs parallel to the courtyard pool into a magical gallery that would become a dramatic, captivating experience at the center of the home. To make the most of the large windows with incredible views, the home's colorations, although quiet and very layered with neutral textures, also needed to highlight and frame the greens of the exterior landscape.

Every surface of the house was touched, from installing patterned reclaimed floors to re-facing walls with beautiful light-reflecting plaster, to lightening and simplifying ceiling details in an embrace of a more timeless and classic sense of architecture. Antique doors were added, reclaimed mantels installed, and previously stained exterior windows and doors were either painted the trim color or finished to feel reclaimed.

Prior to the renovation, the couple didn't spend much time in their formal living room, so one goal of the re-design was to create a space that felt elegant enough for entertaining but comfortable enough to use on a daily basis. Ohara added a TV hidden behind art, and most of the fabrics used for main seating were high-performance or made for indoor-outdoor use. Now it is a comfortable place both husband and wife use to enjoy a special moment while taking in the lovely views.

When building in architectural and reclaimed elements, it is important to have a trusted finisher to blend areas that are damaged or added to when the materials are retrofitted to their new spaces. The same goes for incorporating existing furnishings into a home's new color palette. Pieces that are meaningful, or the right shape and size, can easily be given a new perspective by the right application of a bit of paint.

Finishes are so integral in creating our overall design and sense of lightness. By plastering all of the walls, the light in the house has points of reflection that further the sense of brightness and beauty. Without the palette or the plaster surfaces, the ethereal sense you feel would not be evident.

OHARA DAVIES-GAETANO
DESIGNER

The original den, bar, and kitchen areas were incredibly dark. The cabinets were rebuilt in a white oak and finished to a light neutral, providing the warmth of a natural wood. The custom hood, which was a bit shiny for their taste, was glazed to age its patina. To tie the spaces together, the massive ceiling in the den (opening page) was treated in a similar fashion, creating a coziness to this grandly scaled room. The same tone of lime-based velvety plaster was used throughout the home's main areas, providing continuity and flow while showcasing the homeowners' collected artwork and antiques.

New crown and trim pieces were added to the sides and top of the antique mirrored-over mantel, then seamlessly finished as one cohesive piece.

The home's color palette took a turn in the master suite, complete with a study furnished for both his and her use, and a sleeping suite. Having had the pleasure of creating the seaside tones of the plaster in the couple's California retreat, I was able to bring those same breezy, blue greens to Houston, providing them the soothing feeling that vacation brings all year long. This home, like a beautiful maison located along the coast of France, now has an underlying emotional quality, elegant yet comfortable and inviting.

In the master bath, the design team wanted the existing paint grade trim and casements to look like the whitewashed wood finish we created for the newly built vanities. We were able to emulate the stained finish with a paint treatment, saving the homeowners the expense of replacing the existing wood trims with new stain-grade wood.

SOFT MODERN

DESIGNER BENJAMIN JOHNSTON
ARCHITECT JOHN WAWROSE
BUILDER BROOKSTONE HOMES
PHOTOGRAPHER BENJAMIN JOHNSTON

This Zen-like retreat was designed for a professional couple with small children and an active lifestyle. The space is intended to be a calm, contemporary sanctuary for this busy family, with interiors that draw upon earth tones reminiscent of the seaside. The homeowners envisioned a functional home that felt minimalist but with a sense of layered sophistication. Every step of the design process was taken with this style and their functionality in mind.

The couple have a lot of personality, and this dining room is a perfect reflection of both their style and way of life. The room floods with light from a wall of windows on the north side and a pair of large windows to the west. It also features a two-sided brick fireplace that connects the living room, as well as a pass-through to a large bar—perfect for entertaining large groups. The vision for the space was to maintain the pared-back, minimalist vibe of the house, while creating an unexpected pop of color in the bar area using blue-tinted ombré Venetian plaster. In this home with primarily pale blue walls and sun-bleached woodwork, this dose of textural color is a wonderful surprise. It gives the room a focal point and mimics yet another window to the outside. Guests get to enjoy this feature wall as they wait for a cocktail and as they pass by the bar space toward the formal living room.

We knew that the client wanted the bar space to be a special "moment" as guests experienced the home. And that's certainly what it became. The window into the bar frames a wonderful section of the plaster almost as if it were a painting. In a contemporary space, it's a lovely and welcoming experience to enjoy the perfectly imperfect nature of the embellished wall.

BEN JOHNSTON, DESIGNER

The master bedroom incorporates a muted palette inspired by the tones of the brick on the fireplace. The colors and textures of the plastered walls, woods, and brass accents work together seamlessly to create warmth and comfort—often a challenge in a contemporary space. Pale gray plaster was used throughout the master bedroom and bathroom to contribute to these layers of warmth and texture. Crisp, clean window treatments preserve the minimalist, modern spirit of the space, while sophisticated layers infuse a sense of comfort and luxury for the homeowners to enjoy.

FORMAL FRENCH COUNTRY

DESIGNER TRISHA MCGAW DESIGNS

BUILDING DESIGNER ROBERT DAME DESIGNS

BUILDER ALLAN EDWARDS BUILDER INC.

PHOTOGRAPHER WADE BLISSARD

Kathleen and Daryl loved their Mediterranean-style home, but moving closer to their daughters' school and family church gave them a driving mission to build. They imagined a home where they could entertain their children's friends as well as their own, a generous space where they could welcome their community and host school and church functions. The homeowners were also excited at the opportunity to update their style, imagining a home with cooler tones. The natural exterior stones and soft, blue-slated shutters inspired the interior color palette, with soft neutral backgrounds and soothing blues incorporated into the home's finishes and fabrics. This new, French-inspired design met the couple's desire both for a fresh look and for irresistibly comfortable, engaging spaces to relax and have fun with family and friends.

We looked for ways to personalize and incorporate some of the homeowners' favorite elements from their previous home, such as monogrammed lockers and the mural in the wine bar. These fresh interpretations elicit fond memories of days past.

By plastering the walls in a lovely French blue and stenciling on top with a shimmering pale metallic, a touch of formality was added to this jewel-box room, complementing the antique chest used as a basin.

133

The tile, stone, wood, and specialty finishes became the bones of the home. By layering on color to tie in with fabrics, using stencils together with plaster, and mixing metals, the finishes create a depth of tone, texture, and experience that cannot be achieved with plain paint. Special attention was given to highlighting areas the family sees every day, including the French blue island and pantry doors, mudroom lockers, powder room walls, wine room niche and master bath walls. Antiques from Joyce Horn, found throughout the home, deliver the formal French feel that first inspired Kathleen. The home was completed just in time for Kathleen and Daryl to enjoy those precious handful of years before their girls headed out into the world.

Coating the ceilings and walls of the master bath with waxed plaster both highlights the dramatic shape of the groin ceiling and warms the effect of its cool blue shade. By adding a silver-leaf detail to the glazed cabinetry, the tones of the lighting and fixtures are highlighted, and the job-built cabinetry takes on a furniture feel.

FRENCH WHIMSY

DESIGNER DODSON INTERIORS
BUILDER ELRON CONSTRUCTION
PHOTOGRAPHER JULIE SOEFER

When we think of a spec home, our minds often imagine generic and repetitive. When builder Rona Milbauer and designer Julie Dodson team up, they visualize themselves moving in, so unique tiles, reclaimed elements, and out-of-the-box designs become integral to each project. Having collaborated with this duo for 10-plus years, I am always excited to be a part of their vision, selecting standout finishes for high-impact places.

For this transitional-style home, the team wanted to create fresh open spaces that evoke warmth and encourage comfort, with an easy flow for entertaining. The steel doors and checkerboard flooring separate the entry from the rest of the home while setting the mood for the elegant, whimsical interiors to come. Ceruse-finished oak becomes a statement element for the study and elevator paneling as well as the butler's pantry and wine room cabinetry. Julie furnished the home—chosen for a LUXE showcase— with wonderful art and unique collected furnishings, which elicited a sale during the opening party.

The dining room's eclectic mix of contemporary art, custom chairs and French antiques are set against a bright white canvas. Leading from the dining room to the kitchen, the butler's hall, which also houses a wine bar, has its own unique personality. Wanting a countertop that would complement the finished oak base cabinetry and showcase the intricate mosaic backsplash, the team chose SegretoStone®, as its soft, organic nature adds interest while also marrying surrounding surfaces.

Quarter-sawn beams were installed in the kitchen and breakfast areas, helping to visually separate these spaces from the family room. By applying a thinned primer to the surface, we were able to mask the wood's naturally orange undertones. We then layered the beams with glazes to capture the colorations of the floors and instill a sense of the past into this new build. The kitchen was embellished with a simple inking technique that casts a light shadow on the bead detailing of this Shaker-style cabinetry, creating interest in a clean, subtle way.

The family room is one of my favorites. I love the metal consoles from MAI and the mirrors and architectural fragments that flank them. The custom sofa covered in Twill Sugar indoor-outdoor fabric from Link Outdoor made by The Joseph Company gives the room that extra little detail and whimsy!

JULIE DODSON, DESIGNER

SENSATIONAL SHOWCASE

DESIGNER ELIZABETH GARRETT INTERIORS
ARCHITECT ARCHITECTURAL SOLUTIONS, INC.
BUILDER CUPIC CUSTOM HOMES
PHOTOGRAPHERS WADE BLISSARD,
FELIX SANCHEZ, KERRY KIRK

Working on spec homes is much different than approaching a custom home with an individual homeowner's vision in mind. It's often a challenge to develop truly inviting spaces that will appeal to a wide range of homeowners while maintaining a homey feel. I really enjoyed collaborating with designer Elizabeth Garrett and builder Shane Cupic to infuse this home with beautiful finishes that enhanced the many incredible details these two incorporated into this sensational showcase home. On opening night, one of designer Talbot Cooley's clients made an offer. Talbot then furnished the same home in a wonderfully new and different light.

Elizabeth likes first to envision a home as if she is rambling through it in her mind, taking note of areas where extra details would resonate and engage people's sensibilities. She calls these areas memory spots. This house, built for family life and entertaining, has wide hallways open to large-scale rooms.

The entry way that opens into a spacious living room was one key memory spot. Italian stone, inset into reclaimed wood, set the stage for the beautiful lighting and refined plastered walls that spill over into the formal living room. From the moment you enter the home, softness and elegance feel alive.

Elizabeth is a master of combining old and new. The antique architectural element from Joyce Horn Antiques was repurposed into a console and placed under a contemporary Zhuang Hong Yi work of art from Laura Rathe Fine Art. Constructed from rice paper, it changes color as you move around the piece—remarkable!

The trim in the dining room was painted Benjamin Moore Collingwood to contrast and blend with the plaster. Keeping surface areas neutral in tone allows you to change interior fabrics and furnishings while leaving the backdrops the same, as evidenced by Talbot Cooley's elegant interpretation of the same space.

Wanting the wood for the center island and built-in display cabinets to read natural, we thinly layered multiple glazes over its surface before the final sealer was applied. This masks the yellow and orange tones that most sealers enhance when applied directly to unfinished wood. The perimeter cabinets were painted in Sherwin Williams Worldly Gray to blend with the walls and then enhanced with a dry brushing and edging technique that gives warmth without feeling aged.

The kitchen was another memory spot. An Italian ILVE black-and-brass range and custom vent hood was installed in front of a 16-foot steel window, creating a dramatic art-like statement for the large kitchen-den-breakfast room. By adding reclaimed beams and mixing natural woods with glazed cabinetry, a cozy feeling began to evolve—just the feeling Elizabeth wanted to evoke. Finding a 17-by-6-foot seamless top for the island proved to be challenging. Learning that our new SegretoStone® material could be poured in place—and thus become a seamless counter—was a game-changer. Its organic, sleek appearance balances the dressiness of the hood. The first of its kind installed in Houston, its scale and natural, warm patina give this space the importance this heart of the home deserves.

Talbot designed these unique barstools, which both marry the tones of the wood floors, beams and center island and incorporate the brass in the room. This has become a comfortable, favorite place for the family's children to sit and do their homework.

The butler's pantry marries a Cielo polished quartzite with Davlin rose gold mirrored backsplash tiles. Pulling our inspiration from this beautiful combination of surfaces, the bead details on the cabinets were gold leafed, taking the bar to a whole different level.

Other rooms received special touches, including the stenciled powder room and its metallic finished cabinetry, and the beautiful gleam of the dining room plaster, which was layered with wax and then buffed. At each turn, this grand home pulls you in close with its thoughtful, inviting attention to detail. Memory spots, indeed.

*Finishes are the vehicle that drives our design.
Most of the time we see a particular finish,
and it inspires us to create a design around it.*

ELIZABETH GARRETT, DESIGNER

ETHEREAL ELEGANCE

DESIGNER THE OWEN GROUP DESIGN FIRM

ARCHITECTURAL CONSULTANT
SARAH WEST & ASSOCIATES

ARCHITECT ARCHITECTURAL SOLUTIONS, INC.

BUILDER GOODCHILD CUSTOM HOMES
AND RENOVATIONS

PHOTOGRAPHER WADE BLISSARD

These homeowners wanted to build a new home that would be an elegant, warm space, one with a modern feeling and a natural flow for hosting friends, kids, and philanthropic events. To bring their vision to life, they put together a dream design and architectural team. Sarah West had already worked closely with this couple, whom she now calls friends. Sarah referred her clients to designer Tami Owen to ensure the furnishings and art complemented the clean lines of the architecture and the sleek, artful ambiance the homeowners wanted for the interiors.

The dramatic dining room began with the shimmer in the gray, mottled plaster and evolved by layering silk drapery, a custom cowhide rug, a jewel-like selenite Ron Dier chandelier and a pink-toned painting by Mallory Page from Dimmitt Contemporary Art. The client has a true appreciation for art, so selecting finishes that would showcase their special pieces was a priority.

Entering the family room you are met by floor- to-ceiling steel windows that take your eyes to the clean lines of the pool, hardscapes and beautiful, simple landscaping. Open to the breakfast and kitchen, this room has custom sofas clad in Perennials fabric for worry-free entertaining and a kid- and pet-friendly space for everyday life. Airy drapes with custom rods give a softness and casual feel to the space. The bar/wine room, which hosts sliding reclaimed doors on one side and a statement wall of wine viewed as art on the other, uses SegretoStone® counters that blend with the room's plastered walls while lending an organic feel.

I love keeping a neutral palette with finishes and furnishings so I can add color with art.

TAMI OWEN
DESIGNER

The custom-made charcoal leather barstools, Calacatta honed marble surfaces, simplicity of the plastered hood melding into the plastered walls and ceiling, and the use of mixed metal finishes lend beautiful, understated details to the kitchen, which is open to a sitting room, breakfast area and den.

The powder room, with a steel-and-glass entry door, is both beautiful and unique. Its hallway architecture allows for a private water closet to the right and an open area with an antique, mirrored accent wall and floating sink at the back. With cool, seafoam waxed plastered walls, hand-blown sconces, a contemporary mirror and colorful art, this powder elicits a "wow" from every guest.

Visiting TruStile, a door vendor of The Detering Company, Tami fell in love with both their quality and design. She saw immediately they could create the perfect entrance for this elegant and comfortable master. With soothing plaster running throughout, luxurious bedding, a striking chandelier, and a spa-like bath with a feel of soft powdered snow, this suite offers a spacious, soothing refuge to unwind and relax.

VINTAGE GLAM

ARCHITECTURAL CONSULTANT AND DESIGNER
SARAH WEST & ASSOCIATES
PHOTOGRAPHERS   WADE BLISSARD, PÄR BENGTSSON

When it comes to designers working on their own homes, you often hear the saying, "The cobbler has no shoes." That is most certainly not the case with architectural consultant Sarah West. With her three boys now out of the house, she wanted to add a bit of glamour and a more transitional feel while staying true to the European architectural antiques she had originally incorporated into her abode.

Wanting to create a home with a "fun factor" that lent itself to entertaining at a moment's notice, the designer took her furnishings in a dramatic new direction. From 17th- and 18th-century French to vintage glam, guests are invited to sit in intimate seating vignettes within larger-format rooms. Taking her inspiration from a vintage, ivory velvet egg chair, the home's new design mixes different genres, a technique Sarah calls "architectural/design cross-training." The subtle ivory plaster creates a perfect canvas for the home, softening the backdrop and allowing the reclaimed architectural elements to blend well with vintage Italian lighting and transitional furnishings.

In the living room, as throughout the home, there are deft and welcoming surprises at every turn. Here, the mohair chaise lounges provide an inviting perch for guests to relax while waiting for dinner, or a comfortable place for homeowners to have coffee in the morning. The soft sway of ivory leather fringe on the club chairs immediately entices a guest to a quick swivel.

Sarah removed the walls between the breakfast nook and the living room, and took in the patio from the backyard, enabling her to incorporate floor-to-ceiling iron windows that both expanded the space and flooded it with natural light. The dining room was enlarged in the same fashion, forming a new vignette from an exterior porch. Set against aged stone walls, a custom-designed modern lounging couch covered in pearlized vinyl is a comfortable place for an evening drink or morning look at the newspaper.

In the new layout, repurposed dining room shutters find a new home as pantry cabinet fronts. The pantry has become much more than a storage area—it's now an event to walk inside.

Sarah loves her eight-foot Lacanche range. As she says, "It makes cooking feel beautiful!" The lacquered black range, with a brass backsplash and contemporary SegretoStone® hood, balances the hand-scraped and limed wood kitchen door fronts and reclaimed stone counters, striking just the right balance of old and new. The antique oak linen press found in Marché Paul Bert in Paris, used for ample seating and prep and serving surfaces, has been topped with a milky marble slab to add a more transitional feel.

171

*If you have the right person helping you make timeless,
educated decisions, the word "challenge" soon comes to
mean a fabulous adventure!*

SARAH WEST, DESIGNER

MEDITERRANEAN REVIVAL

DESIGNER JJ DESIGNS

ORIGINAL ARCHITECT FRANCIS BURRALL HOFFMAN

RENOVATION ARCHITECT RAY FENTON

BUILDER BALL CONSTRUCTION

PHOTOGRAPHER JEAN ALLSOPP

Finding the perfect beachfront getaway home, one that would be a refuge for their children and growing number of grandkids, took Kathy and Craig on a six-year hunt. They settled on the charming town of Boca Grande, a small, tranquil residential community on Gasparilla Island where there are no condos, where shop owners know you by name, and people get around on golf carts and bikes. But after seeing countless homes, they had yet to find their perfect fit. Hearing of an off-market home that might be sold to the right buyer, the couple went to take a look. They pulled up to the walkway, and before they even had a peek inside, Craig turned to Kathy and said, "This is the one." Fortunately, the current owners agreed.

This 1920s home, designed by the notable architect Francis Burrall Hoffman, had cypress windows, hardware, and wood-detailed ceilings. Although beautiful, the house's unique history and flair came with some big challenges. Built in an era of formal entertaining and living quarters for servants, the kitchen was small and closed off. The couple knew they would need to make big changes to make this historical home work for their lifestyle. Kathy, who owns JJ Designs with her daughter Heather, was excited to make this storied home her family's retreat. Together, mother and daughter envisioned transforming the home's elegant yet simple characteristics without losing its original beauty.

Early on, Kathy hoped the finishes could help restore to the home the character it once had. So, we boarded a plane together and set off to make her vision come to life. The original plaster had been painted over repeatedly and now just looked like paint. After many layered applications of varnish—and years of smoking in the rooms—the wood trim, doors and ceilings were dark, orange, and flat. Wanting to lighten and brighten these dark spaces, we picked a refreshing plaster tone to re-coat all the interior surfaces and refinished the wood to its initial intent.

Originally the grand hall entrance had a coat closet which you had to walk through in order to get to the powder bath. Rumor has it that during Prohibition the family hid their liquor behind a hidden panel in the powder bath, to keep their stash safely concealed. This pass-through coat is now the home's formal powder, featuring a beautiful statement Italian antique sink and mosaic inset into an antique mirror.

The new kitchen and dining areas were created by taking in a servant's bedroom, half-bath, laundry, and screened-in porch. The kitchen was the main focus; the rest of the floor plan evolved from there. The previous dining area, with its breathtaking views of the beach, was transformed into a sitting area, which is now open to the home's interiors. The china cabinets were constructed from the doors of the original kitchen's glass-front cabinetry. By matching the finish of the old with the new wood, these past treasures found a place in the home's updated design.

The plaster in the master suite took its color direction from the bath's beautiful, waterjet, mother-of-pearl tiles from ADR. It has become Kathy and Craig's favorite place to sit on the porch and watch the sunset.

———————

The outside was brought to life by painting the stucco Benjamin Moore Ballet White. The shutters, painted Sherwin Williams Reflecting Pool and then washed with Sherwin Williams Meander Blue, created the most beautiful seaside shade. The woodwork, both inside and out, was cleaned, re-stained and brought back to its original splendor.

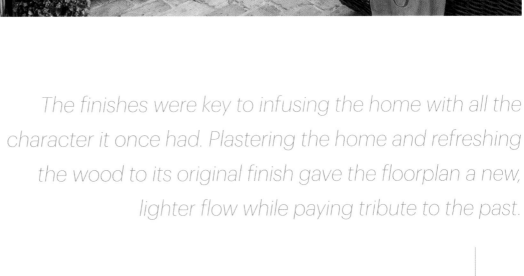

The finishes were key to infusing the home with all the character it once had. Plastering the home and refreshing the wood to its original finish gave the floorplan a new, lighter flow while paying tribute to the past.

KATHY JOHNSON

TIMELESS
MEDITERRANEAN

DESIGNER KARA CHILDRESS, INC.

PHOTOGRAPHER WADE BLISSARD

Lori and her husband purchased this classic Mediterranean home in love with its location and hoping to update it with a modern freshness that would accommodate their passion for entertaining. Lori hired Kara Childress to fashion an interior with a timeless, understated style. Hearing that these two talented, fun women were working together, I knew their collaboration would be a perfect fit. Lori is an accomplished designer in her own right. Kara has a gift for creating effortlessly comfortable, sophisticated interiors that engage and entertain family and friends.

I met with Kara and her principal designer Ally Dougherty at the house to select a plaster tone that would pull the more taupe colorations from the existing floors. A runner was added to the staircase, and doors to the library were custom-made and upholstered with a "hair-on-hide," creating a soft entrance to the high-sheen room. For the trim we selected Sherwin Williams Accessible Beige to lessen its contrast and blend with the plaster, giving the home a more modern feel. By using natural fibers such as linens, wools, mohair, cottons, and many perennials, the home feels luxurious while providing durability for this family with kids and two cute Jack Russell pups, Chip and Olive.

Incorporating the original door of a famed Houston cigar bar into the library was a special request from the husband. Papering the ceiling in a snakeskin-embossed wallcovering, and finishing the vents to match allow the fun, eclectic vibe of the room to not be distracted by utilitarian necessities.

A muddy palette lends warmth and age throughout the home's central areas, with pops of color added to the offshoot study and dining room. The dining room's subtle wall covering was dramatically enhanced by the rich tones of the glazed woodwork and the lush silk draperies. Layering the room with an antique chandelier, a modern Kelly Wearstler mirror hung above a balcony-railing-turned-console, and plenty of whimsical art bring to life the welcoming ambiance Lori wanted for her many dinner gatherings.

The home is filled with textural subtleties. In the formal living room, the fabric inset that showcases the focal 17th-century Flemish tapestry is softened by a row of antique journals placed on the mantel. The large custom chandelier and high-impact modern art help to scale the 24-foot ceilings, creating a coziness in this grand space.

The glazed cabinetry in the kitchen is anchored with antique, reclaimed Belgian bluestone pieces, creating indestructible counters for daily meals and buffet entertaining.

Because you look through the bar opening in the entry and see the pantry doors, the team decided to create a finish that would make these previously white doors feel reclaimed. Layering them with texture and glazing them in the same teals used throughout the home created an interesting focal point for a space where hanging art was not an option.

191

The vintage concrete floor tiles from Chateau Domingue inspired the tones of the powder's plastered walls. Mixing an antique chandelier and sconces with modern art and black-and-white photography is the perfect blend of old and new.

The den has beautiful natural lighting, ample cozy seating, and a game table where this couple often enjoys their favorite game of backgammon. The custom, ceruse-finished oak coffee table by Zach Elkins and layered rugs from Creative Flooring add more cozy sophistication and textural interest. The chandelier introduces an antique element to a very modern space.

MODERN YORKSHIRE COUNTRYSIDE

DESIGNER, FURNISHINGS ALLYSON TRACY PLUMMER
DESIGNER, HARD SURFACES TRACY DESIGN STUDIO
BUILDER MONTECITO BUILDERS
PHOTOGRAPHER WADE BLISSARD

Wanting a livable home where their grandchildren and their two pups would be welcome in every space, Debbie and her husband fell in love with this home's big open spaces, which would be comfortable for family gatherings. They were delighted by the hard surfaces and color palette slated for this Yorkshire-inspired spec house already in progress, and this modern take on the English countryside became a wonderful starting place for the home's interiors.

Although a traditional English home brings to mind patterns and strong tones, Debbie and designer Allyson Tracy Plummer wanted a cohesive mix of traditional and modern for the interiors, in keeping with the home's open concept and light-filled rooms. The colorway for the furnishings evolved naturally, pulling tones from the light, hand-scraped wood floors, brick accent walls, limestone counters, and the Belgian bluestone flooring. Rugs from Madison Lily evoke a sense of modern in a soft way, allowing the traditional lines of the linen and chenille-upholstered pieces and antique furnishings to combine beautifully with the more contemporary accessories and art.

When I was called in to collaborate, the home was complete and beautifully furnished. Both Debbie and Allyson loved how it had evolved, but felt something was missing. As I walked the home and listened to Debbie talk about how she entertained, how she cherished the days when her grandkids came to play, and how she felt about her two beloved pups, Cade and Fidder, I had a sense of the missing element. Each room, with its soaring ceiling heights, opened up to one another. It gave the space a gracious, light and airy feeling—but it also exposed a lot of painted, light sheetrock, which can feel cold. We decided to plaster the most lived-in areas of the house. Although applied in the same tone as the original paint color in the home's main areas, the plaster gives more depth and slight variation to the walls. This finish supplies the warmth and emotional resonance Debbie had been missing.

A few other areas received customized treatment. The dining room's paneled accent wall was glazed to combine the colorations in the tapestry chairs with the newly acquired contemporary rug. We used this new tone to plaster the surrounding walls along with the graceful oval dome, creating soft transitions between elements. By editing the finishes in the space, we were able to showcase the furnishings and beautiful drapery treatments.

The barely lavender plaster tone in the formal powder bath offsets the room's reclaimed tile flooring and unique sink basin, infusing just a hint of color to the space.

The master suite was transformed into a calming space, where Debbie feels enveloped in beauty and tranquility. The color chosen for the plaster had a tinge of blue gray, which plays off the upholstery, bedding, rugs, window treatments and marbles. The result? Walls with a soft, almost movement-like quality.

STATELY ELEGANCE

DESIGNER CHANDOS INTERIORS

RENOVATOR GOODCHILD CUSTOM HOMES
AND RENOVATIONS

PHOTOGRAPHER LAUREY GLENN

Purchasing the home nearly two years ago, this couple now knew how they moved through it, lived in it, and what they wanted it to be. Clear on what they wanted, the time was right to renovate. With keen eyes for art, a love of entertaining, and a vision for a home that was cosmopolitan and inviting, the homeowners asked Chandos Dodson Epley, who had helped them with their Colorado home, to transform their Houston residence into one of elegance and comfort.

Originally designed with a cottage feel, the homeowners wanted the look of a fabulous London townhouse, where striking contemporary art shared space with fine antiques. Luxurious fabrics, artisan-made furniture and refined finishes would create additional layers of sophistication, depth and interest. Chandos spent the better part of the week on her own in New York scheming and sourcing. The homeowner joined her for three full days of modern and contemporary art auctions at Christie's, Sotheby's, and Phillips.

The clients had come to love living with plaster in their Colorado getaway. When it came time to renovate their Houston home, they requested plaster for all the walls and ceilings of the house. Seeking a high degree of refinement and a showcase for statement lighting and art, we chose a smooth white plaster for the home's public spaces that was quiet, almost porcelain like. The dining room is elegant without feeling stuffy, a place for the homeowners to linger with guests long into the night. The formal living room is also designed for sophisticated entertaining. Here, the contemporary art sets the tone. A Kate Shepherd oil and enamel on wood panel from Hiram Butler Gallery hangs in the formal living, as does a Gael Stack mixed media canvas from Moody Gallery. The family room is elegant while still being comfortable and inviting; the designer took her starting point from the deep, rich color of the antique rug.

In the master, a warm blue plaster on the walls and ceiling separates this room from the rest of the home's colorations creating a cozy, pared-back, European feel, full of quiet details. The elegant bath is coated in a polished white plaster, enhancing the barrel detail of the ceiling and complementing this room's luxurious lighting, marbles and statement slipper tub.

The finishes make this already interesting home even more interesting. Every surface has a personality. It feels much more sophisticated and warm.

CHANDOS DODSON EPLEY, DESIGNER

207

FRENCH ACADIAN

DESIGNER LUCAS/EILERS DESIGN ASSOCIATES, LLP
ARCHITECT CRAIG STITELER DESIGN
BUILDER K&C CLASSIC HOMES
PHOTOGRAPHER JULIE SOEFER

As empty nesters, logic told them to downsize. Instead, when Jaime and her husband found a larger spec home under construction and close to the city, they decided to customize it and make it their own. They wanted comfort and space, with ample room to accommodate their three boys' growing families with grand-dogs in tow. They loved the rustic French exterior of the home, as well as the large kitchen that opened to a family room and fabulous outdoor entertaining spaces.

Excited but unsure about where to begin, Jaime gathered her magazine inspiration photos and a copy of my design books and set an appointment for us to meet at the job site. The home was in sheetrock stage, and during our walk through we came up with a wonderful plan for finishing, starting with the most beautiful blue for her kitchen cabinetry. The house had many wonderful elements already chosen, such as the reclaimed beams and the pine flooring salvaged from the American Crayon Company in Ohio.

I always thought I wanted white cabinets, but after looking through wood finish samples at Leslie's showroom I fell in love with a blue faux finish and, of course Leslie tweaked it "a little," and then it was perfect!

JAIME, HOMEOWNER

Recognizing that some of the other selections in surfaces the builder had made were not in line with her tastes, I suggested Jaime work with a designer to help her customize the hard surfaces, lighting, and furnishings to reflect her vision. With construction already well underway, Jaime hired Sarah Eilers, and they began a whirlwind tour of shops and showrooms to formulate a design that would fulfill Jaime's dream of timeless interiors with contemporary art accents. Jaime loved being a part of the design process. She was involved every step of the way. With Sarah and project manager Laura Beth Rickaway, the trio created the home's color palette using the rugs, art, and fabric as inspiration.

The main home was kept neutral in tone, and we chose richer plasters and warm cabinet finishes for the study, dining room, powder bath and master retreat to set those rooms apart. Jaime's husband, chiming in for his study, wanted stained tongue and groove boards on the back of the shelves and glazed painted fronts. Using these finishes for inspiration, the walls were coated in a rich plaster and then waxed with a walnut stain to add a warm patina to the space.

The powder bath has a color palette all to itself. After finding an antique French chest, its tones were used for the bases of the plaster, offsetting all the antique elements in the space.

The large-scale playroom sits over a three-car garage and features four draped, built-in bunks that create private, cozy nooks for grandchildren to read and sleep. Not knowing if this delightful space would be for boys or girls, primary colors were chosen, inspired by the colorful Jim Thompson fabric used for the ottoman and curtains.

The spacious master suite was coated in a soothing blue plaster, taking its color
inspiration from the warm draperies, cool marble, and polished nickel fixtures in the bath.
A mix of antique and contemporary lighting, beautiful artwork and a few unexpected,
sentimental pieces came together to make a warm, comfortable, family-focused home.

A TUSCAN VIBE

DESIGNER TRIANGLE INTERIORS
BUILDING DESIGNER COLBY DESIGN
BUILDER GOODCHILD CUSTOM HOMES
AND RENOVATIONS
PHOTOGRAPHERS RAY PEREZ, WADE BLISSARD,
MICHAEL HUNTER

Inspired by the many villas and farmhouses they saw on their countless trips to Italy, Natalie and Brett wanted to recreate the warm feelings they had experienced when walking through Tuscany's old-world interiors at home. Lovers of life, their vision was to build a place where they could easily host their slew of family and friends and be the house where their four children's playmates always felt welcome.

Collaboration with their team was crucial for this couple, and they were both joyfully involved in the building and design process. They encouraged open communication and creative dialogue from what they call their "dream team"—a group the homeowners say was instrumental in successfully building a large-scale home that feels intimate and welcoming, incorporating both vignette "play" spaces and expansive rooms for family and friend time. Designer Nicole Zarr has a genius for maximizing seating without making spaces feel crowded. Here, she created ample places for family and guests to visit as well as open walkways so large parties can easily meander from room to room.

After meeting at the home with Nicole, we customized a plaster to pull the neutral warm tones of the home's natural stone walls, creating a restful backdrop that flows through most of the home. Thoughtful finishes transformed job-built cabinetry into custom furniture pieces, a design element that was crucial to this home's evolving style. We aged surfaces—including the added wood necessary to retrofit reclaimed doors, and surrounds and furniture used as bath vanities—to contribute to the illusion that the home was built centuries earlier.

Incorporating Natalie's Tobago heritage, Nicole added a touch of the island vibe and pops of color throughout. The hand-painted floors in her office lend a casual, fun feel to the space, balancing the vibrancy of the orange grasscloth wallcovering and hot pink furnishings.

In a nutshell, I would say that the finishes took the home from incredible to exceptional. It's one of those things where you can't—or don't—appreciate the incredible impact until you see it done, and then it's very much a "WOWZA" moment. Talk about the cherry on top!

NATALIE, HOMEOWNER

The master suite has become a sanctuary where Natalie and Brett end their busy days in a dreamy, spa-like retreat. The plaster, which hints of lavender, has soothing undertones and glows as the lights reflect off its slight sheen. Natalie describes it with one word: "delicious." The bedroom's beams, which were originally painted white, seemed too stark for the room's dreamy feel. A soft glaze was added, subtly distressing them to further heighten the romance of the space. The silver leafing on the bead detailing of the cabinetry enhances the jewel-like hardware and beautiful slipper tub.

HISTORY
REINTERPRETED

ARCHITECTURAL CONSULTANT AND DESIGNER
SARAH WEST & ASSOCIATES
BUILDING DESIGNER ROBERT DAME DESIGNS
BUILDER PARKER HOUSE, INC.
PHOTOGRAPHER WADE BLISSARD

Wanting a family home with space to welcome frequent visits from their grown children and host events for their philanthropy, this couple decided to build. Guided by their deep appreciation for the history and character of elements from the past, they hired architectural consultant Sarah West to incorporate antique and reclaimed features into their new home and bring their vision to life.

Entering the front door through a lush courtyard garden, large steel windows provide breathtaking views of the flowers, greenery, and stately old oaks that surround the home. Walking in, you are met by open hallways that expand into rooms, providing the most wonderful flow throughout the home.

The plastered walls and ceilings, along with reclaimed flooring from West Virginia and Kentucky, provide an authentic canvas for all the antique built-in elements and furnishings. In the entry, those include an 18th-century altar from Touraine and a massive, 17th-century stone surround that leads to the sunken wine room.

The stair treads created from full slabs of antique wood felt disconnected from the newly constructed black staircase railings. Softly layering the wrought iron with umber and gray glazes instilled a newfound patina that marries both elements to the same era.

The sunken wine cellar is complete with a custom-designed and beautifully showcased tequila bar. Seeking a more rustic, aged feel to this space, we applied Domingue Architectural Finishes plaster, which is imported from Belgium.

The great room, which expands into the kitchen and breakfast areas, incorporates beams taken from a structure on the family's own South Texas ranch, 18th-century doors from Avignon, and a stone mantel from a farm in France's Lorraine region. Sarah incorporated multiple large-in-scale seating areas with comfortable transitional furnishings, creating cozy vignettes for everyday living and ample seating for large events. By creating pieces that combine old and new, such as the coffee table made from a piece of salvaged architectural glass set on a brass base, history is reinterpreted with a modern perspective.

When purchasing reclaimed doors and other elements, often the finish is not quite perfect, or you may have to add new wood to the existing materials. Don't worry! The shape, style and size are the most important; colors and textures can be changed, like the many we refinished in this home to work perfectly in each space.

In one of my favorite treatments to date, new wood planking was installed, then plastered over, sanded back, glazed, and waxed to lend the most beautiful finish to this charming back powder. To complement a beautiful antique basin, the front formal powder walls were limewashed in a faint basket-weave pattern. With this technique it is very important to properly seal the walls so that water splashing from the faucet does not stain the finish.

In the kitchen, the statement island, a 17th-century cabinet from a French sacristy, was reworked using its original shelving to create storage drawers and doors for the organized cook. By housing the day pantry and refrigerator behind newly constructed doors that we custom finished to lend age, the kitchen is reminiscent of a chef's workspace in an historic château, but with all the modern conveniences of today.

By integrating 18th-century French shutter doors into the plaster walls, a beautiful focal point is created that also hides shelving within the framing of the walls. This typically unused space now houses the homeowner's large collection of vintage pottery, without protruding into the room. An 18th-century Italian chandelier hangs above an 1830s Swedish rococo table that has been modernized with a marble slab top. The butler's pantry, with antique mirrors as countertops, has ample storage under the draped linen skirting. Using the same plaster wall treatment throughout allows special elements to be showcased while keeping a warm and sophisticated flow.

Without plaster as a canvas, my vision of creating rooms with history, character and carefully integrated transitional details could not have been believable.

SARAH WEST
DESIGNER

The master suite includes beautiful courtyard views and his and her baths. By mixing vintage, antique, and transitional elements, the furnishings reflect the past, present, and future.

The found iron grates Sarah envisioned for her bath cabinets were rusted and a bit too rustic when combined with the marble counters and nickel fixtures. After cleaning, glazing, and applying a worn silver leafing detail they now work beautifully, backed with antique glass. To balance the old in hers, his new shutters and hardware were finished to feel aged.

BEAUTIFULLY ECLECTIC

ARCHITECTURE AND DESIGN NEWBERRY ARCHITECTURE

BUILDER GOODCHILD CUSTOM HOMES
AND RENOVATIONS

PHOTOGRAPHER LAUREY GLENN

Finding a tucked-away lot with beautiful views, these homeowners decided to build. Warm, inviting and fun, they wanted to create a home that reflected their personalities and enabled their love of casual, frequent entertaining, with ample space for their kids to have friends over and room for their large extended family and friends to enjoy. Eclectic in style, they formed a design and build team who are as thoughtfully creative as they are. The clients and the team embraced this opportunity to let their imaginations run wild, while keeping a measured eye on how every detail interacts with the others that surround it. The result is rare and remarkable synthesis of different touches and textures, which allow a unique blend of materials to offer surprises without overwhelming the eye.

With large-scaled rooms, floor-to-ceiling steel windows and doors, and wide openings, the home's flow is natural; you ease from one space to another. The softness of the plaster showcases the colorful palette of the furnishings and art, lending a subtle depth and cohesiveness that cannot be achieved with plain paint. "The plaster has movement, but it doesn't compete with any of the furnishings," says designer Gina Brown. To instill a warm, lived-in feel to the home, Gina chose a reclaimed wormwood flooring from Turkey and artfully deployed it throughout, playing with different patterns to define spaces and create interest.

Entering the home, you step right into a room with colorful art and club chairs and a fireplace flanked by a folded, pink-hued paper and anchored with a blush SegretoStone® hearth and plastered walls and ceiling. Immediately, you're enticed to pause, sit for a visit, and enjoy the space. Off the entry, the dining room employs a colorful wallcovering on the ceiling and features a blush leather custom chandelier, pulling tones from the whimsical chair fabric and soft, airy feel of the drapery.

By painting the cans and vents to blend with the colorful wallcovering, your eye is not interrupted with blocks of white, and statement pieces in the room are highlighted without distraction.

The family room, with two seating areas layered with rich textures, feels curated and intentional. One side (cover page), clad in wood and painted with a high-sheen finish, is a conversational area. The other, perfect for family movie-watching, is centered around a soaring, arched custom hutch, transformed into a TV cabinet and finished to work in its new space. The reflection from the pool off the plastered ceiling showcases the custom brass light fixture, which was templated and laid out on the ceiling first, before its construction began.

With the feel of an old working kitchen, this hub of the home is a culmination of interest and refinement. Shiplap walls, two-tone paint, and board-and-batten ceiling highlight the featured hood, a reclaimed altar piece from a monastery that was flipped upside down and finished to feel as one found piece. To incorporate a pastry shelf into the island, a stainless steel, brass and acrylic shelving unit was customized, lending ample room for storage. Faced with the Turkish flooring, and ended with a walnut butcher block, the layered textures contribute to one splendid, cohesive space.

So not to obstruct the exterior views from the breakfast room, a banquette-style couch and comfortable chairs were custom designed in colorful fabrics and set beneath an overscale light fixture with translucent fabric to infuse a light and airy feel to the space. The exterior fireplace is a combination of the home's painted brick, a reclaimed timber and a natural, concrete-toned SegretoStone® facing. These very simple architectural statements let the owners' pieces, which are beautifully vibrant and strong, come forward.

The master bath, intended to feel like an original farmhouse structure, has been modernized and elevated with rift-sawn white oak wood, a matte plaster, custom floating brass mirrors, marble inlaid flooring and elaborate hardware and fixtures.

ASTRONAUT RANDY BRESNIK

LIFE AFTER HARVEY

I have lived in Houston for the majority of my life and have always felt at home. Living here, I have experienced a deep connection to the city's multicultural dynamic and friendly, down-to-earth values. Hurricanes are part of life here, just as the risk of earthquakes, fires, snowstorms, or tornadoes exist in other parts of the country. Hurricane Harvey was different from other storms. It affected all our neighborhoods and touched every part of the city. For once, the media did not overstate the devastation. The images we saw of people rising to that challenge have been imprinted in our memories for years to come.

I certainly felt the storm's rage: trying to get my crews working in Midland home to their families on the last flight able to land in Houston, learning the home I grew up in had flooded, and grieving with, and for, many friends and staff members close to me who lost all they owned. There isn't a single person I know who was not shaken by the storm in some way. The courage, compassion, and gratitude I saw firsthand was a testament to the goodness in all of us, and a reminder that regardless of our backgrounds, we are all connected. This was Hurricane Harvey's silver lining and legacy. From the people whose situations were dire, to the heroic first responders, to just plain old people helping people and neighbors helping neighbors, living through Hurricane Harvey has been a reminder of the strength of individuals and the power of a community when we all pull together. Houston has a fierce tenacity to survive and flourish, and we who live here are forever thankful to those around the nation who so selflessly contributed their time and money to our city's survival.

Two years later, we are still rebuilding. All the trades have joined together to give those who lost their homes a new hope for the future. It has been an inspiring journey for me to create spaces that engender excitement for those who have lost their homes and furnishings and instill a feeling that their new house is home. I want to share some of their journeys and inspire you with their positive outlooks on life, as that is what home is all about.

A BIT OF SHIMMER

DESIGNER TRISHA MCGAW DESIGNS
RENOVATOR PINNACLE CUSTOM BUILDERS
PHOTOGRAPHER WADE BLISSARD

Laura and Mark spent 24 years raising three children in a home they remodeled five times, each evolution creating an ever-more perfect fit for their family and their lifestyle. Then Hurricane Harvey arrived. After they left Houston to escape the storm, their home filled with three feet of water that did not recede for 10 days. While the swift actions of a dear friend helped save a few priceless rugs, jewelry, some art, and a handful of other precious possessions, their beloved family home was ravaged. Mark and Laura made the heart-wrenching decision to find a new space they could again make their own.

Mark immediately saw the potential in the new house, with beautiful traditional moldings and great backyard views, in a neighborhood the couple loved, but Laura wasn't as sure. The couple turned to designer Tricia McGaw to create an elegant, livable space that struck a balance between comfort and sophistication, with a shimmer of Hollywood glam.

As we worked together to select the finishes, Laura's sense of excitement blossomed. Selected treatments throughout helped achieve the balance of traditional and contemporary, formal and easygoing, that reflect the homeowners' sense of relaxed elegance. By widening the opening between the living room and dining room and reversing their use, they were able to incorporate a bar and serving space. Wanting these front areas to be special, the walls and ceilings were adorned with plaster, the existing granite fireplace surround replaced with SegretoStone®, and the curved brick ceiling in the bar lime-washed. Echoing the fresh and comforting colors of the plaster, the trim and walls were painted Sherwin Williams Crushed Ice throughout the rest of the house.

Lighting, both natural and artificial, is essential to creating the right setting for this couple. The transformation included new doors and windows throughout the downstairs that gave the house a more modern feel and allowed abundant views of the outdoors. Although most of the lovely light fixtures are new, three pairs of sconces salvaged from their old home found a perfect fit in their new one.

The curved brick ceiling in the bar was lime-washed to soften its harshness while allowing variations in the brick to subtly show through.

Removing a staircase that separated the kitchen/breakfast area from the den opened the kitchen to the generous family room. This gives a sense of flow and expansiveness, and provides the homeowners with a necessity for them: an inviting, elegant, functional space to host family and friends. Accessorized like a living space, the kitchen brims with surprise and the thoughtful marriage of beauty and functionality. Mirrored doors on the Sub-Zero refrigerator are a beautiful way to disguise the appliance, incorporating it into the room.

In the kitchen, a more accessible pantry is enclosed with new custom doors that were finished in an aged and beautiful, soft, blue gray to feel reclaimed. The same tone, glazed with a different technique, was repeated on the kitchen island. Repeating the plaster used in the front of the home on the kitchen hood provided consistency weaved throughout the home, and a cost-saving alternative to plastering the entire room.

Among a handful of possessions salvaged from their old house? A painting of mine the homeowners purchased years ago. It now hangs in their family room above a SegretoStone® cube table. I was so touched to see it give them joy in their new home.

LESLIE, SEGRETO FINISHES

UPDATED CLASSIC

DESIGNER ELLIE BALE
ARCHITECT JOSHUA I.F. JONES
BUILDER GOODCHILD CUSTOM HOMES
AND RENOVATIONS
PHOTOGRAPHER WADE BLISSARD

Sometimes the best things in life are the most unexpected surprises. They were feeling perfectly content with their current house when a realtor friend called Ellie and David to tell them about a home on the market designed by the famed architecture firm of Lucian Hood. The couple hadn't been thinking about moving, but they were intrigued. They decided to take a look. At first sight, they fell in love with the home's classic lines and the lush grounds characteristic of Houston neighborhoods located on the ravine. The home was built in the '70s and the original owner had not made updates. Ellie knew she had a project in store. After hiring architect Josh Jones to draw the plans and Steve Goodchild to construct their vision, Ellie became her own client, designing a home for her family.

Living just down the street from Ellie's home, I loved seeing the new changes each time I walked the neighborhood. The Georgian brick exterior was dressed with a fresh coat of paint and larger rectangular windows. Adding a stone surround gave the exterior a refreshed curb appeal. I helped Ellie with her previous home, which leaned toward Country French, and I was excited to see her plan for the interiors.

Before

After

After contemplating many bold treatments for the formal powder, the decision was made to keep it elegant and simple. The walls were plastered and the antique cabinet was painted in a high sheen and embellished with gold leaf paper to incorporate the tones from the mirror, fixtures and sconces into the piece.

Meeting after the sheetrock was installed, we discussed her vision of a welcoming home, furnished with antique, modern, and sentimental pieces and filled with her collection of whimsical art. Ellie showed me the rich textures with pops of vibrant colors that she'd chosen for fabrics and wall coverings. We began to devise a plan. To make the white walls feel special, the two-story entry was plastered, lending both depth and polish. To maintain visual continuity, the floors were replaced with wide plank walnut and the ceilings in the living and dining spaces received the same white plaster as the entry, while the walls were given a personality all their own.

While most people are opening up walls, in this home the large living area across from the dining room was partially closed, creating a formal study for her husband, and the upstairs library was completely walled off to provide an upstairs bedroom for their son. The study took its inspiration from a wallcovering, which is inset into wood framing. To create an interesting paneled effect in the room, we painted the trim Benjamin Moore Shoreline, and glazed it to enhance the wallcovering it bordered.

Before

After

Inspiration for the dining room came from the fabric "Brighton Pavilion," part of the Miles Redd Collection from Schumacher. The softest tone was pulled from the fabric and plastered onto the walls, creating a soothing palette to calm the bright fabrics and contemporary art. The butlers pantry, painted in Sherwin Williams Cloudburst and enhanced with a gold leaf detail, extends the tones of the dining room and adds visual interest to the pass-through space. The rest of the home was painted Sherwin Williams Alabaster, which showcases the stunning marble surfaces, brass hood, and hardware. All the doors in the home were painted in a high-gloss black and dressed with beautiful brass hardware, creating an interesting accent.

After

Before

275

Before

*I want people to come in to our house
and feel like it's their own.*

ELLIE BALE, DESIGNER & HOMEOWNER

The sunken living room created a bit of a hazard—a lot of people were missing the step. To draw attention, an elongated diamond pattern was painted directly on the wooden step, to add an interesting detail while also putting safety first. Sadly, this room flooded after Harvey and the step had to be redone, as did the bar cabinetry. Ellie and Dave have an army of friends and they love to entertain. Their home reflects all the ease, grace, and welcoming spirit with which they live.

Before

After

The beautiful bar cabinetry, first glazed, has a painted brass detail that emulates the chic bar shelving unit. The Lucite and brass barstools taken from their previous home were refinished from chrome to brass. Many furnishings can be reinvented in a different light by just applying a bit of paint!

CLASSICISM MEETS MODERNISM

DESIGNER DON CONNELLY

ORIGINAL ARCHITECT AYNESWORTH

RENOVATION BUILDING DESIGNER COLBY DESIGN

RENOVATOR KERR CONSTRUCTION LLC

PHOTOGRAPHER WADE BLISSARD

This home was well built, with large rooms, high ceilings, and great bones. Located on the Bayou, it had an amazing backyard and a view that deserved to be showcased. The interior was very traditional with heavy drapery, dark mahogany wood, and lots of paneling. The homeowners wanted a sleek, modern-but-transitional look that would blend with their existing antiques and their vision for an inviting, updated aesthetic.

It wasn't until the homeowner met Don Connelly that her dream for this traditional Georgian home was understood. She had seen Don's work before, and had visited his store, Area, so she knew his flair for mixing sleek contemporary with antiques would be a good fit for her. Struggling with the creative process, she had Don walk through the home. He saw its potential and understood the homeowner's vision before she did. The design transformation began.

Walking into the entrance, the staircase to the right, your eyes were pulled through a vestibule to a grand, dark-stained paneled room and landed on beautiful views of the lush ravine. Sensing that the main living area's color palette would direct all color decisions throughout the home, Don came to our showroom armed with a rug sample and a few fabrics for color inspiration. The homeowner, unsure of how to move away from her past traditional style, brought a heavily glazed cabinet sample and photos she had taken from luxury hotels during her many travels. Listening to Don, and walking her through some more refined finishes, we settled on a color direction and suggested she add a silver leaf detail to the bead molding in the paneled living room, infusing some glam into this large space.

The sample for the paneling, which was approved at our next meeting, had a full glaze that altered the original base color. We selected Sherwin Williams Aesthetic White to blend, which became the direction and color palette for the entire home. The cigar foyer (seen on the previous page), with its stunning mosaic floor design, acts as a vestibule to the formal powder and has views of the verdant, flourishing garden. To further heighten the room's drama and showcase the crystal chandelier and vaulted ceiling, a pearl wax was used over a light-toned Venetian plaster, making a sophisticated yet quiet statement.

Starting with brass inlaid marble mosaic floors, the powder evolved to be a shimmering jewel set within the home. The room was adorned with a Phillip Jefferies wallcovering, luminous crystal fixtures and a beautiful vessel sink. Our job was to give the cabinet equal importance by enhancing its design and incorporating all the room's colorations in the finish.

I believe I understood the beauty of this home when the paint and finishes came into play. Amazing how that was a game changer! Segreto completely changed the look of these dark spaces, and it was then that I got excited about what this home could be.

HOMEOWNER

The products chosen for the hard surfaces needed to be beautiful and highly functional and to wear well over time. Quartzite counters, which don't etch or stain like marble, and beautiful mosaic tiles were used for the kitchen, bar and butlers. Porcelain, which looks like natural stone without the maintenance concerns, was selected for outdoor hardscapes. Neolith tiles made from crushed stone are beautiful, lightweight, and heavy duty, a perfect choice for the floors in the kitchen. Marble and onyx were used in limited places with an awareness that they stain over time. The electrical plates on all of these stones were painted to emulate the surfaces they rest upon so their beauty was not visually interrupted, creating one seamless elegant feel.

This transformation brought ah-ha moments and unexpected turns every single day. In the midst of the renovation, Hurricane Harvey hit. Three times during the makeover, the homeowner wanted to sell this home. A turning point came when the expanded glass windows and doors were installed. That's when the cozy, open feeling the client had been longing for without even knowing it came to life. With the outdoors now flowing in, she realized it was not someone else's home anymore. It was her own. She experiences great joy waking up in the morning, overlooking the ravine through the large master bedroom window, then walking through the Bayou Room to the breakfast area, where she's greeted with another amazing view.

Sitting in that breakfast room, in peaceful solitude, with beautiful vistas and her first cup of coffee, is the gift of living in this home—one she enjoys every morning!

BRINGING THE OUTSIDE IN

DESIGNER MARY JANE GALLAGHER INTERIOR DESIGN, MICHELLE STEWART DESIGN
RENOVATION ARCHITECT CUSIMANO ARCHITECT
RENOVATOR KERR CONSTRUCTION LLC
PHOTOGRAPHER WADE BLISSARD

Whenever I drive by, this house has always made me pause to admire its charming architecture and beautiful lot located at the end of a cul-de-sac that backs up to the Bayou. Although I had been in the home to consult with a previous owner, I had no idea it was a classic John Staub. During Harvey, the water rose over 50 feet and 14 inches of water flooded the home's first floor, causing all to be lost. Although devastated, like most Houstonians the homeowners moved forward with a positive outlook, taking this as an opportunity to create a new look and fresh space for their active family of six.

Designers Mary Jane Gallagher and Michelle Stewart had both worked with homeowner Beth on previous homes. Beth knew the pair could make her latest vision real: bringing the outside in and giving the home a natural, fun and elegant feel.

After creating a statement in the family room with Gracie's Ivory Silhouette wallcovering, the team felt the mantel should be both simple and high impact, while also serving as a distraction from the television. Black stone was used for the recessed elements of the piece. The box was framed, covered with sheetrock and then plastered and waxed in a color that pulled the background tones of the surrounding paper and created a luster to set it apart.

During the remodel, the library fireplace was uncovered—a surprise discovery—and restored, and we created a simple plaster surround in the same fashion.

With the exception of the lighting, which survived the flood, the entire kitchen was rebuilt. The French oak cabinetry was wire brushed to raise the grain and given a series of glazes to read as though untouched while infused with tones of the floors and the whites of the Calacatta marble countertops and walls.

A RETREAT
ON THE RAVINE

DESIGNER JENNIFER RIGAMONTI
RENOVATOR DOYLE CONSTRUCTION
PHOTOGRAPHER WADE BLISSARD

Located on a ravine surrounded by a lush forest, Lisa loved the feel of this home from the moment she stepped through its front doors. "It felt like a treehouse!" she recalls. Beautiful as it was, the color palette and ultra-traditional style of the home were not her own. Lisa is a founder of DASH Market, a curated shopping event with dealers of mid-century modern, contemporary, industrial, and retro-vintage treasures. She had no trouble visualizing this home with new finishes and the soothing tones that resonate with her sensibilities.

The house had amazing floors and a great floorplan. Free from the need to make structural changes, Lisa was able to immerse herself fully in a design transformation. I was brought on board to explore the possibilities new finishes could bring. Having worked with Lisa on her previous home, I was returning for a second time to work with this dream team: Lisa, her designer Jennifer Rigamonti, and builder Jim Bob Taylor. Our collaboration was an expression of pure teamwork and so much fun to be a part of.

Selected areas were given special treatments, such as a light neutral plaster in the entry and dining, a dramatic blue Venetian in the powder, and fireplaces toned to remove their gold undercurrents. The kitchen received a complete cosmetic facelift with a transformative finish on the cabinetry and new SegretoStone® counters.

In the powder, the dramatic walls are coated with Venetian plaster. The vivid walls and eclectic décor mix contemporary and old-world elements. The mirror over the mirror is brilliant. The first one is wall hung and the second attached from the ceiling using fishing wire. Architectural consultant Sarah West was instrumental in bringing in unique reclaimed elements into the home, such as this reclaimed sink.

The work that Segreto did on the surfaces was instrumental in making our new home our own. Although beautiful when we bought it, the colors that bring me joy were not represented. So, we changed the "lipstick" and made it feel like home.

LISA, HOMEOWNER

The kitchen, which was a dark stained wood, was lightened dramatically through a series of glazes that allowed the grain of the wood to show through. Replacing the center island and bar with a new plaster SegretoStone® countertop enabled the rest of the perimeter counters to remain as is. The island received a textured finish to further heighten its furniture quality and set it apart from the rest of the cabinetry.

With comfortable upholstered barstools, the kitchen island has become a favorite place to eat, sit and sip on morning coffee, and enjoy a glass of wine after a busy day. The adjoining den has become a family gathering place with multiple seating areas, a game table, and baskets of toys for their adored pup, Katie Lady!

Before

The perimeter cabinets were originally stained in an orangish tone. In moving to a taupe, we were able to maintain the stained look without stripping them first. The color inspiration? The stunning new tile from Chateau Domingue behind the range.

KITCHENS

Inspired ideas to encourage
community and create
lifelong memories.

Lyndsey, the lady of the home, undertook an exhaustive search to find the right designer to transform her family's newly purchased French-style home into the eclectic aesthetic that had captured their imagination. Happily, that search ended when designer Lindsey Herod was brought on board to bring their vision to life. Lyndsey authors the fashion and lifestyle blog L. Avenue, has three young children, and loves to cook and entertain, often hosting beautiful dinners and curating the events herself, right down to the elaborate tablescapes.

Here, open shelving was installed for easy access and the cabinets were painted a deep emerald green, providing contrast for the new marble countertops and backsplash and setting off the unlacquered brass hardware. It was exciting for me to watch this kitchen take on a fresh, new perspective, and to see the soft white plaster on the walls, ceilings and hood create a sculpture-like effect that's both striking and subdued. Lyndsey's SegretoStone® breakfast room table, purchased for a previous home, has found a place in this new breakfast space. Now, this kitchen is not only the heart of this home but also a dramatic statement room, and exactly what the homeowners wanted.

DESIGNER *Lindsey Herod Interiors* **RENOVATOR** *Goodchild Custom Homes and Renovations*
PHOTOGRAPHER *Laurey Glenn*

Wanting to create a statement in this kitchen, Sarah West incorporated a floor-to-ceiling art wall of reclaimed tile that offers a unique perspective for this space. Mixed with aged brass pendants, clean-lined, Shaker-style cabinetry, contemporary hardware and a waterfall island, the plaster tone used throughout the home coats the hood, ceilings, and perimeter walls, enabling flow and merging elements in this open floor-plan kitchen.

ARCHITECTURAL CONSULTANT *Sarah West & Associates* BUILDING DESIGNER *Rice Residential Design L.L.C.* BUILDER *Abercrombie Custom Homes, L.P.* PHOTOGRAPHER *Wade Blissard*

This typical ranch had been through many revisions with previous owners. The new homeowner had a clear vision that her kitchen should be comfortable and inviting and hired Whitney Janke, founder of Nest & Cot, to brighten and transform the space to be full of function with a clean European feel.

One never knows where they will find their starting inspiration. Spying a French altarpiece during a shopping trip to Joyce Horn Antiques, Whitney immediately knew this would be a beautiful focal in the kitchen. Turning it upside down, she was able to use it for the kitchen hood with little modification. With open shelving reclaimed from a pottery studio, concrete counters, and a newly built furniture piece that was finished to read like an antique, the kitchen has an open feel, with ample storage. To further enhance the French farmhouse feel, the cabinets received a full glaze to soften their appearance and allow them to blend with the reclaimed elements in the space.

DESIGNER *Nest & Cot* PHOTOGRAPHER *Wade Blissard*

With their love for entertaining family and friends, it was important to Pam and Patrick that their kitchen be both well-organized and beautiful. Because the kitchen is open to formal areas, designer Suzanne Duin was challenged to create an elegant and uncluttered space that complemented but did not compete with the surrounding rooms. The plastered surfaces, glazed cabinetry, touches of brass, and quartz slabs all work together to add a more formal, polished look to this most used place in the home.

DESIGNER *Maison Maison Design* ARCHITECT AND BUILDER *Butler Brothers* PHOTOGRAPHER *TK Images*

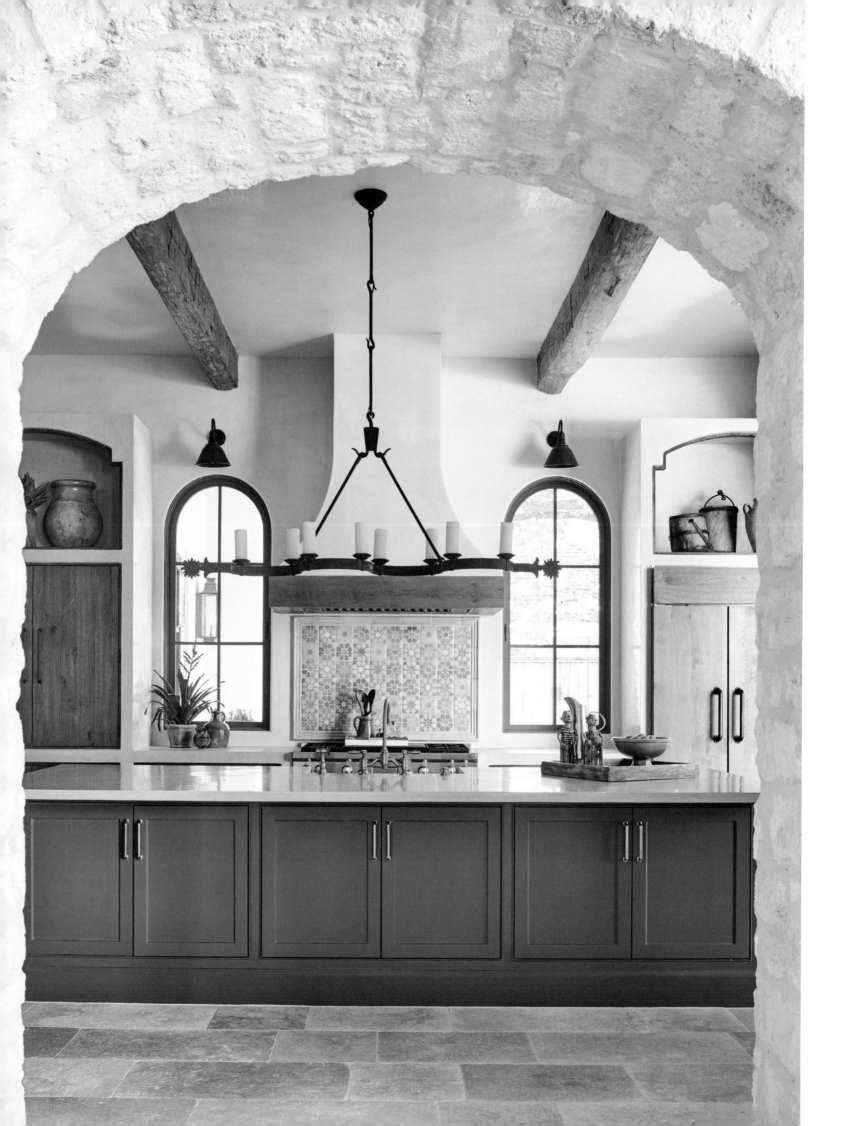

Traveling with her husband over the years, Linda loved the warmth and interest of European design. Waiting for a time when she could focus on building her dream home, over the years she collected photos of just what she wanted to accomplish. That time arrived, and with pictures in tow, Linda and designer Cindy Witmer came to our showroom to see just how finishes could add to her reclaimed elements, sleeper beams, and unique tiles. Plaster was chosen to give an authentic backdrop to the home's Mediterranean architecture. Linda fell in love with SegretoStone®, and her cabinet boxes, tops and styles were framed in wood and covered in hardy board, allowing us to coat the surfaces with our signature plaster. This produced an effect of reclaimed wood door and drawer fronts inset into solid plaster boxes. Timeless and organic, this technique lends the sophisticated warmth and casual feel Linda wanted in this most-used place in her home.

DESIGNER *Cindy Witmer Designs* BUILDING DESIGNER *Robert Dame Designs* BUILDER *Stonehenge Classic Homes Inc.*
PHOTOGRAPHER *Laurey Glenn*

The homeowner's wish was for "a room that functions as a kitchen," not a kitchen per se. To grant that wish, we combined French country farmhouse details with thoughtful antique touches as a nod to the home's storied past, in a newly open and more functional space that enables a large family to gather.

JOSHUA JONES, ARCHITECT

This charming home, nestled in the quaint town of Brewton, Alabama, was built in 1938. As in many historic homes, there was only a small working kitchen connected to the dining room by a narrow butler's pantry.

At every holiday and family get-together, the topic of conversation would eventually turn to how to update and expand the kitchen to better accommodate gatherings of extended family and friends. This went on for about 15 years until a recent Easter dinner, when Susan's son quipped, "If you ever do this renovation, what will we have to talk about?"

She began the demolition the following week. Rather than a narrow, built-in island, a table was placed at the center of the room, in keeping with the farmhouse style. This generous, inviting station provides additional counter and serving space as well as a seating area to dine or visit with the cook.

DESIGNER *Stanley Ellis Inc.* ARCHITECT *Joshua I.F. Jones* RENOVATOR *Daniel Johnson, D.H.I.* PHOTOGRAPHER *Laurey Glenn*

The cabinets were totally rebuilt while the range, sink, and refrigerator—the working triangle—although replaced, stayed in their original locations. The bead detail on the gloss-black base cabinets was embellished with gold to complement the CornuFé range, and the oak cabinetry above the range was designed with a furniture flair to hide the exhaust fan and provide additional storage. Inspired loosely by the French farmhouse aesthetic, millwork elements from the original butler's pantry were incorporated, existing steel-cased windows were painted gloss black, and a Shaws Original sink was installed.

Faced with the challenge of an existing concrete subfloor that couldn't be removed and didn't allow enough depth to install wood or tile, we painted a checkerboard tile pattern, creating a beautiful, cheerful floor and solving the problem of keeping the back-entry floor level with the wood kitchen.

Pulling from her childhood summers visiting family in Europe, Natalie's vision for her own home was to create an inviting space for friends to gather, with a clean feel and an old-world influence. Evoking the sense of serenity when surrounded in white, the marble counters, hand-done subway tiles and plastered hood bring together varying textures of the same tone. Envisioning a functional island, Natalie wanted a handcrafted table feel to the piece. The natural quality of the SegretoStone® island top complements the perimeter marble and grounds the distressed finish applied to its base. The bull head, representing an old French boucherie, welcomes all people who visit the cook. A kitchen focal, it pays homage to Natalie's dad and grandfather, who were skilled butchers at the local grocery store.

DESIGNER *Maison Blanche Design LLC* ARCHITECT *Rice Residential Design L.L.C.* BUILDER *Bella Torre Homes*
PHOTOGRAPHER *TK Images*

Armed with her vision of a modern Belgian farmhouse, Selina hired Beverly Shaeffer to redesign the footprint of this traditional 1960s ranch style kitchen into one which opens to the den, better serving her love for spontaneous get-togethers. A reclaimed concrete tile found on a discovery trip became the kitchen focal wall and the inspiration for the color palette. Plaster was chosen for the walls and ceilings, giving the illusion of height to these spaces. The focal island, topped with SegretoStone®, received a textured finish to balance the tile, lending a furniture feel to the piece. In order to achieve the look of antique stone floors for less, three types of limestone and travertine were ordered in varying sizes and finishes, creating uneven surfaces and chipped edges that emulate the patina and old-world feel of those from an 18th-century French chateau.

DESIGNER *Beverly Shaeffer* RENOVATOR *Justo & Company* PHOTOGRAPHER *Wade Blissard*

This is a uniquely transitional home, with an open floorplan kitchen and many beautiful elements. Amid the slurried brick, striking decorative tile wall, pendant lighting and drop-down wooden counter seating, it was crucial that the hood's statement be found in its simplicity. Keeping the inset design architectural, the hood was plastered in the same tones as the walls, creating a soft detail that did not overshadow the other beautiful elements of the space.

BUILDER *David James Custom Builder*
FURNISHINGS *Talbot Cooley Interiors*
BUILDING DESIGNER *Robert Dame Designs*
PHOTOGRAPHER *Kerry Kirk*

Redesigning this ranch home for her clients, designer Sarah Eilers combined a fresh, diverse mix of traditional and contemporary styles that reflect this large family's deep Texas roots. It was important that the remodeled kitchen maintain an open concept, include a large island for gathering, and have ample counter space. Live-edge wood shelving along the steel-framed windows showcases the breathtaking views and allows natural light to pour into the room. The glazed cabinetry and contrasting walnut and soapstone countertops come together to create a warm place for family and friends to gather.

DESIGNER *Lucas/Eilers Design Associates L.L.P.* ARCHITECT *Natalye Appel + Associates*
BUILDER *Jefferson Christian Custom Homes* PHOTOGRAPHER *Julie Soefer*

Mural by **SEGRETO**, *Designer* **CLAUDIA LUMMIS**, *Photographer* **LAUREY GLENN**

BATHROOMS

|

Create a refuge that will relax your
soul, allow you to unwind and refresh
your start to each day.

————

Setting out to remodel one of the oldest farmhouses in Houston's Piney Point Village, Walter and Layla wanted to preserve its farmhouse feel, with a French Country design that relies on a few timeless, fundamental elements to maintain a consistent visual aesthetic throughout the home. In the master bedroom and bath, Layla, with friend and designer Rily Suffel, looked to infuse elements reminiscent of the couple's favorite boutique hotels. In the master bath, they started with a closed-in, yellowed space that was home to a hot tub, and went on to completely re-invent the space. To open up the room, the windows were re-worked and walls of glass were used for the shower and toilet areas. Marble tiles and concrete counters were installed, and sheetrock surfaces were plastered in a warm, white tone, showcasing Layla's own photography. New storage and custom mirrors helped the space achieve a sleek and soothing feel. This beautiful master bath now allows the homeowners to wake up every morning feeling as though they are on vacation.

DESIGNER *Riley Suffel* RENOVATOR
Goodchild Custom Homes and Renovations
PHOTOGRAPHER *Wade Blissard*

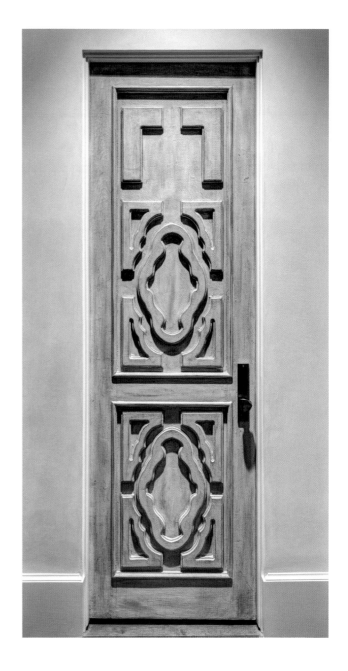

With interior trends giving design the freedom to mix different styles and periods, finishes are often employed to meet the challenge of blending elements or juxtaposing modern with old world. In this powder designed by Sarah West, the SegretoStone® counters, lighting, and contemporary, raised-plaster wall treatment infuse a sense of "the present" alongside the antique sink and reclaimed concrete floor tiles. The intricately designed door received an aged, textured finish, creating an art piece and a sense of importance in this statement room.

ARCHITECTURAL CONSULTANT *Sarah West & Associates* ARCHITECT *Rice Residential Design L.L.C.* BUILDER *Abercrombie Custom Homes, L.P.* PHOTOGRAPHER *Wade Blissard*

ADJACENT IMAGE

Creating an interesting combination of old and new, designer Ken Kehoe tiled this front powder's focal wall with mirrors then created layers of gold accents with the framed mirror, faucet and sconces. The custom designed and built door and sink vanity received an aged finish, giving a warmth to their chic backdrop. Further enhancing the space, gold leafing embellished the basin's details, unifying the elements into one elegant space.

DESIGNER *Ken Kehoe & Company* BUILDER *Cupic Custom Homes* PHOTOGRAPHER *Wade Blissard*

OPPOSITE IMAGE

The Baguès-inspired sconces led the concept for Pam's formal powder's design. By mirroring the back wall and setting a slab marble floating sink in front, the number of different elements and materials were kept to a minimum. This creates a bigger impact in a small space than incorporating a furniture piece, sink and wall-hung mirror. Pulling tones from the marble, the walls were blanketed in a soft gray plaster, adding another level of sophistication to this already elegant space.

DESIGNER *Maison Maison Design* ARCHITECT AND BUILDER *Butler Brothers* PHOTOGRAPHY *TK Images*

I feel that children's rooms should be designed with longevity in mind. Pretty in a soft pink, the space is sophisticated and glamorous, a place that this little one's adult version will also love.

TRISHA MCGAW
DESIGNER

Dry brushing and edging the vanity, and adding a metal leaf paper to the bead detail of the cabinet fronts, tie together the golds of the fixtures and jewelry-like pulls. Because we seal all our finishes with an acrylic polyurethane, they are not only beautiful but also are durable and will not yellow over time.

DESIGNER *Trisha McGaw Designs* BUILDING DESIGNER *Robert Dame Designs* BUILDER *Allan Edwards Builder Inc.* PHOTOGRAPHER *Julie Soefer*

OPPOSITE IMAGE

This powder bath was inspired by a single, unique piece. The console used for the sink vanity came from the homeowner's mother. We formed a concrete top that followed its shape, and it became the focal element to the room. With the belief that there should be but one star, the walls were left quiet and coated in a soft plaster.

DESIGNER *Nest & Cot*
PHOTOGRAPHER *Wade Blissard*

ABOVE IMAGE

Armed with her vision of a modern Belgian farmhouse, Selina hired Beverly Shaeffer to redesign the footprint, manage the construction, and consult in selecting new surfaces and finishes. When the wall separating the shower from the vanity area was removed, the master bath was completely transformed. Using an image found on Pinterest as inspiration, we finished the custom-built cabinetry, and plastered the shower and surrounding walls with Tadelakt plaster, creating a seamless look that enlarges the space visually and invokes the style the homeowner loves.

DESIGNER *Beverly Shaeffer* RENOVATOR *Justo & Company*
PHOTOGRAPHER *Wade Blissard*

Taking her inspiration from an article she read about a new high-end condo in San Antonio's Pearl District, Linda fell in love with these patterned concrete tiles. Researching the source, she found Redondo Tile, which became the starting inspiration for her master bath. The walls were plastered to dress the space and a charcoal glaze was added to the raw wood cabinetry, creating a softer, more Zen-like effect than what the same color in a straight paint could achieve.

DESIGNER *Cindy Witmer Designs* BUILDING DESIGNER *Robert Dame Designs* BUILDER *Stonehenge Classic Homes Inc.* PHOTOGRAPHER *Laurey Glenn*

OPPOSITE IMAGE

To complement a beautiful antique basin, the front formal powder walls were limewashed in a faint stripe pattern. With this technique it is very important to properly seal the walls so that water splashing from the faucet does not stain the finish.

ARCHITECTURAL CONSULTANT AND DESIGNER *Sarah West & Associates* BUILDING DESIGNER *Robert Dame Designs* BUILDER *Parker House, Inc.* PHOTOGRAPHER *Michael Hunter*

ABOVE IMAGES

Starting with beautifully scaled architecture, a decorative glass tile from Ann Sacks became the inspiration for Elizabeth's design. Placing them behind the vanities, which were inset into curved niches, created a feature accent wall that balanced the room's ceiling height. As the square footage in this room was vast, to stay in budget the decision was made to focus on cabinetry finishes. An aged gold leaf applied to its bead not only enhanced their design but enabled the mix of metal-toned hardware, lighting and mirrors to work well in this lovely master bath.

DESIGNER *Elizabeth Garrett Interiors* ARCHITECT *Architectural Solutions, Inc.* BUILDER *Cupic Custom Homes* PHOTOGRAPHER *Wade Blissard*

Sallie, who was designing this home for her son, daughter-in-law and two grandsons, wanted the powder to reflect the lady of the house's feminine side. Incorporating all of her daughter-in-law Sherri's favorite tones, she had flowers and birds hand-painted on the walls to open up the space visually and create a beautiful oasis in a home that is typically filled with boys. Murals can be customized to preference and budget, and are not only one of a kind but also a more affordable alternative to hand-screen wall coverings.

DESIGNER *Sallie Davis* ARCHITECT *Architectural Solutions, Inc.*
BUILDER *D. L. Doyle Construction*
PHOTOGRAPHER *Wade Blissard*

Inspired by various London hotels and bars, Sheri, who was both the homeowner and the designer, let her English roots influence this Texas scaled powder room. Appealing to her rebellious side, the black and white elements of the mosaic tile felt a little rock and roll, while the warm golden tones allowed for a soft transition where the tile met the hallway's reclaimed wood. Taking our cue from an intriguing wall covering, a one of a kind, layered, matte Venetian plaster was softly applied to complement but not overpower the statement elements of this lovely room.

DESIGNER *Bailey Vermillion Interiors* BUILDER
Goodchild Custom Homes and Renovations
PHOTOGRAPHER *Wade Blissard*

Inspired by the London Ritz, Claudia Lummis wanted this penthouse unit in a Houston high-rise to feel as if it were an elegant London townhome. Layered with antique fixtures, pink onyx mosaic flooring and solid slabs used to form the tub skirt, shower surround and countertops, a beautiful custom blush paint was formulated for the paneled surfaces complementing the stone. Originally, only the cabinetry was slated to have a refined glaze in a richer shade of the same tone. However, when starting the project and seeing how beautifully the paint enhanced the onyx, I suggested instead to treat the paneling and cabinetry as one, adding gold leafing to the bead details on all the woodwork. To finish off the space, a dramatic ceiling was hand-painted in a trompe l'oeil fashion, emulating a luxurious fabric trimmed in gold braid. A town home in the sky, this project (with photos taken before the homeowner moved in) was such a rewarding collaboration between the design, architect and build teams.

DESIGNER *Claudia Lummis* ARCHITECT *Dillon Kyle Architects* BUILDER *Windham Builders* PHOTOGRAPHER *Wade Blissard*

Plaster fluting by **SEGRETO,** *Prototype designed for* **MARIE FLANIGAN INTERIORS**

INNOVATIONS
& CREATIVE
SOLUTIONS

Constantly challenged to elevate the
level of architectural finishes, Segreto
is passionate about coming up with
innovations and cost-saving solutions that
will create beauty in the lives of our clients.

THE JOURNEY TO ALWAYS CREATE

Sometimes I wonder, do I just get bored easily? Whenever the company seems to be manageable and I start to contemplate the concept of balance in my life, that's right when I tend to dive headfirst into something new. At first, I thought this was a way to deal with empty nest syndrome. When my oldest child, Matthew, went to college, I opened an art gallery. I had so much fun working with and mentoring young artists. They inspired me to paint myself. I began to carve out time and discovered how much I enjoyed mixing paints, plasters and textures to create canvas art. To my surprise, they sold. When my second child, Kirby, went off to school, I opened a retail space within our studio. It was fun to go to market and to try to predict what people would find unique and appealing. Kirby joined me on many of those buying trips, and they were a wonderful mother-daughter experience. With Sammy, I decided to self-publish a book. I absolutely love to learn, and honestly, when it came to writing and putting together a book, I was starting from scratch—what a learning experience these books have been! It's been tremendous fun to share many of the projects we are so blessed to be a part of, and to open people's hearts to the ways beautiful surroundings can enrich our lives.

Passions come in all sorts of forms. One of my great passions is trying many different things and never allowing the creative process to end. It has been my gift and my joy to work alongside so many artisans and talented staff members. The newest journey I've embarked on? To allow my dedicated, gifted, visionary team to grow, take charge, and bring Segreto to a place where the company runs without me. I tell my clients I will be around for the next 20 years. But creating space for these talented young people to lead has turned out to be my most challenging and rewarding journey of all. Thanks to their assistance, passion, and drive, here are a few of the new ways we are now able to personalize homes and add beauty to our clients' lives.

OPPOSITE IMAGE

First hand-formed from clay, molds were then cast to create these lovely florals that were organically applied to the ceiling, fashioning a beautiful, dramatic raised effect.

DESIGNER *Shann Kastendieck* CLIENT
Valobra Master Jewelers
PHOTOGRAPHER
Wade Blissard

Deciding she wanted a worry-free change where she could just lock up and go, designer and artist Diana Humphrey purchased a shell in a new Houston high-rise and set off to create her own oasis in the sky. Diana's vision was to use meaningful art, clean lines, minimal but inviting furnishings, and a dash of the unexpected. I've worked with Diana for almost 20 years, so I was excited to catch up with her and to bounce ideas back and forth. Great restraint is required in creating a soft, contemporary home; the backdrop here needed to be both quiet and artistic. The room was coated in white plaster with a soft sheen, and the bed wall was transformed into a piece of art with a low relief technique, forming a grid of white-on-white rectangular shapes. The effect creates a subtle, enchanting visual statement.

DESIGNER *Diana Humphrey* ARCHITECT *Robert Levy + Associates* CONTRACTOR *Goodman Even Inc.* PHOTOGRAPHER *Laurey Glenn*

The design and placement of fixtures, cabinetry and art in a contemporary home is like an artist creating a still life. Each object plays off the others in size, height and shape, and is significant to the overall beauty of the final painting. In a home, like in a painting, this arrangement must offer visual joy.

DIANA HUMPHREY
DESIGNER

The soft colorations of the master bedroom continue into the spa-like master bath. In this room, the focus was on combining functionality and beauty while editing each element. At the vanity we applied a wall of waterproof Tadelakt plaster, simplifying the space by negating the need for a backsplash. There's a wonderful element of surprise and fun in the irregularly shaped white handmade sculptured rocks made from our SegretoStone® product, which rest at the base of the fiddle leaf fig.

I didn't want the home to feel too modern or cold, and the scalloped plaster accent wall created a warmth and interest that plain paint couldn't achieve.

DAVID JAMES
BUILDER

Creating a home for clients that was also going to be a LUXE showcase home was a chance for builder David James to do something different. A creative in his own right, he wanted the finishes to be crisp and clean while also giving warmth to the space. Originally thinking he would create a fluted accent wall out of wood, after meeting with our design team, David's vision changed to plaster, which lends a softer feel to the home's linear, open architecture.

BUILDER *David James Custom Builder* **FURNISHINGS** *Talbot Cooley Interiors* **BUILDING DESIGNER** *Robert Dame Designs* **PHOTOGRAPHER** *Kerry Kirk*

SEGRETOSTONE®

It came as little surprise to me that Kirby, my creative child, became a designer. But I insisted she work for someone else before she decided if Segreto was the right place for her. After three years of working for an interior design firm, Kirby felt it was time to come on board. She appreciated the diverse scope of design aesthetics that we tackle. Once a part of the team, she jumped right in, coming up with some fresh new finishes for our design offerings. Kirby was enjoying herself, but at a staff meeting one day, she confessed: she missed designing furniture. I suggested that she revive that creative love and develop her own line for Segreto. Isai, my operations manager, who is very creative himself and is a master at figuring out how to build just about anything, chimed in. "Why don't we revitalize the plaster material we were developing for countertops and reinvent it into a furniture line?" From that concept, SegretoStone® was born.

SegretoStone® is composed of an all-natural, lime-based plaster that is poured over a solid concrete, wood, Hardie board or stone base. It's then polished to a luminous luster to produce a finished material that is both beautiful and durable. Our stone's quiet, organic surface has subtle variations and a soft sheen, which mixes well with other surfaces and melds with any design style. We started with dining and coffee tables with unique Lucite bases and have evolved the line to include custom fireplaces, counters, sinks, outdoor loungers, water fountains, doors, lighting and much more. Available in 20 signature colors, SegretoStone® offers unlimited options in size. Unlike natural stone slabs that are usually 60 square feet or less, SegretoStone® can be fabricated seamlessly for extra-large areas such as kitchen islands and dining tables.

DESIGNED BY *Leslie Sinclair, Kirby Sinclair* **PHOTOGRAPHERS** *Wade Blissard, Pär Bengtsson*

Just as a personal stylist would curate a wardrobe to complement an individual, I took this home's design and created it in a way to best complement and suit Erin and her family.

SHANNON CRAIN
DESIGNER

This updated take on traditional design incorporates personal touches that echo homeowners Erin's and Rickey's personalities and reflect their current stage of life with young children. They hired Shannon Crain for the second time to create a sophisticated home that supports play, offers durability and combines beauty and function. The warm tones and textures of natural materials are intermixed with shades of blue and green, keeping the room fresh, light and inviting. The fireplace made from SegretoStone® became a sculptural element in the space, bridging the gap between the mix of transitional, contemporary and traditional elements.

DESIGNER *Shannon Crain Design*
BUILDER *Riverway Development, Inc.*
PHOTOGRAPHER *Kerry Kirk*

Although the majority of our projects are residential, I couldn't say no when designer Marie Flanigan and Cathy Lam reached out to me to discuss finishes for Lam Bespoke's second home furnishings showroom. Both women are friends of mine, so I knew this would be a fun collaboration—and after all, this space needed to feel like one big home! It was fascinating to hear Marie's vision of turning a large empty shell into a showroom that would feel like multiple vignettes of a home.

Selecting texture-rich materials was key for Marie. We were challenged to form a large plastered wall in which the store's logo was carved. That wall now creates a quiet but dramatic statement as you walk into the showroom. In an exciting first for us, for this project we used our newest SegretoStone® product, a plaster made from lime that has been infused with fibers and aggregates, which creates a stone-like surface when dry. This same lime plaster was used for the counters on top of the layered, distressed cabinetry we finished for the checkout counter. Though the store's overall palette is understated and neutral, the layering of textures, including rustic, wide-plank European oak flooring, sleek steel windows, and romantic sheer drapery panels, conveys a rich patina and tactile interest.

DESIGNER *Marie Flanigan Interiors*
CONTRACTOR *Midway*
PHOTOGRAPHERS *Julie Soefer, Wade Blissard*

We never tire of classic color combinations, and black and white is a definite firm fave! It's a look that whispers clean and sophisticated.

MARIE FLANIGAN
DESIGNER

I love how the men and women's powders take the same fundamental elements—here, a mirror, sconces, and floating sink—and use finishes to achieve such utterly different looks. The choice of finish takes you to dark, elegant, and dramatic, or to light, simple sophistication. The floating sinks are formed from slate and natural tones of SegretoStone®, one of our 20 new colors for the line.

PHOTOGRAPHER *Julie Soefer*

SEGRETO PAINT

In creating interior finishes, selecting the right tone is at the forefront of every decision we make. I am drawn to the soothing palettes that our plaster finishes embody; I love how they inspire relaxation in living spaces. Plaster's subtle variation and reflective quality is a big part of the soothing quality are its finish. After customizing and personalizing colors for so many unique projects, I now understand just how much the tones themselves play a role in establishing the feelings a finish evokes.

Beautiful rooms are a culmination of textures, scale and materials that all work in harmony, seamlessly and without one overpowering the others. The backdrop plays a crucial part in the success and overall feel of any room. Determined to make the most of the power of finishes to contribute to the impact of a space, I began formulating my own colors for clients, both to blend with our plasters for trim and to apply in surrounding rooms. Experimenting with colors on wooden boards, I would take my creations to the paint store to be mixed into gallons. Many times, I found that their formulations did not match what I'd created. In order to better serve our clients in the quest for perfect ambiances, we have embarked on a new adventure. We're developing our signature soothing tones in paint for everyone to enjoy. I'm almost never more comfortable than in jeans, with a paint brush in my hand, so this process has been a lot of fun. I started by mixing colors in plastic cups with Andrea, one of my talented designers. We formulated 50 colors to start, which we manufactured into our own line: Segreto Paint. Through our ongoing work to customize "the perfect color" for so many of our clients, we have added 52 additional colors to our portfolio. Comparably priced to other affordable brands, it is our joy to have developed shades that inspire tranquil surroundings for all to experience.

PHOTOGRAPHER *Pär Bengtsson*

Designer RACHAEL MICLETTE
Renovator MORRISETT CONSTRUCTION
Photographer WADE BLISSARD

NEW USES FOR AGE-OLD MATERIALS

Known as the first true paint, this limewashing has protected ancient monuments, European cathedrals and historic museums. Limewash is made from limestone that has been crushed, burned and mixed with water to make a lime putty. The putty is aged and then thinned with water and colored with natural pigments. When used over brick, stone and concrete, it is absorbed into the masonry without trapping moisture and has a chemical makeup that removes odors and harmful carbon dioxide, improving interior air quality.

Lending a depth and luminosity to flat walls, brick and stone, this artistic application can be applied to create many different effects, all mottled and matte with a chalky, nuanced texture. The beauty of lime? As it ages, it develops unique patterns and shadings. Over time it leaches white, lending a sun-bleached look. In its base form, limewash is white. Color is achieved by adding natural, alkali-resistant pigments, which are available in shades dictated by what the earth has to offer. Keep in mind that limewash becomes up to 10 times lighter as it dries, so it's important to test colors before committing. The opacity depends on the number of coats applied and the amount of water used to thin the product.

With patience and care, you can paint like the ancients—and enjoy the same enduring results.

DESIGNER *Garrett Hunter* ARCHITECT *Michael T. Landrum Inc.* BUILDER *Sawyer Enterprises* PHOTOGRAPHER *Wade Blissard*

We have had great success transforming the coloration of brick or stone while still maintaining its natural feel. In this home the past owners definitely had a Mediterranean, old-world style. The lush fabrics and darker ambiance created a home that had a very formal feel. The new owners, more casual in style, loved the home's architecture but preferred a less-is-more aesthetic and a light, bright interior. All the main areas were plastered, and the stone and brick in the house was limewashed. Seeing the transformative power of what finishes could do, the homeowners asked if the same process could neutralize their exterior stone. The answer was yes, and the outcome was remarkable.

BUILDING DESIGNER *Robert Dame Designs* BUILDER *Abercrombie Custom Homes, L.P.* PHOTOGRAPHER *TK Images*

Kitchen After

After

Kitchen Before

Before

DEVELOPING
A PLAN

When building or renovating your home, how do you decide where to place the finishes that will inspire your vision, evoke your personality and enhance your way of life? Many of us cannot transform every surface at once. Here's how I encourage homeowners to approach this big design question. Select the special places that will make the biggest impact in your space, and give those areas top priority. At the same time, create a long-term implementation plan for what you ultimately want to achieve with finishes throughout your home. These two important steps will ensure your home always feels complete and future additions will flawlessly evolve. Starting in this home with plain walls and millwork, carefully selected finishes were chosen to create an inviting atmosphere to the dining room and enhance the cabinetry, instilling a custom feeling throughout.

While wanting child-proof interiors, this family of five's vision for their home was to create timeless, sophisticated spaces where ease of entertaining was paramount. In creating a plan to plaster their home in stages, it was decided the dining room—where dinner parties are frequent, festive occurrences—was a perfect place to start. Many people are concerned about stopping and starting plaster where cased openings are not trimmed in wood. As you can see, meeting at the inside edge of the dining room, the plaster and the straight paint achieve a natural flow. The dramatic, graphic, hand-painted floor design not only makes a statement in this room but also provides easy cleanup if guests spill on the floor. The cabinetry on either side of the artful wine room is coated in an acrylic sealer infused with metallic powder to relay the soft illusion of shimmering silk.

DESIGNER *Leslie Strauss Interiors* BUILDER *Bentley Custom Homes*
PHOTOGRAPHER *Wade Blissard*

Decorating around the realities of humans, kids, and red wine isn't easy. However, textiles have come a long way, and stains can be easily cleaned with soap and water. Today's fabrics can be life-changing, in how we design and decorate. I used performance fabrics everywhere in this home. My favorite right now is Crypton.

LESLIE STRAUSS
DESIGNER

In the kitchen, where cabinetry has more square footage than walls, we decided that painting the walls and trim Benjamin Moore Decorator's White and glazing over the cabinetry base of Sherwin Williams March Wind would create the biggest impact, including enhancing the statement tile used for the backsplash.

Centered around a Phillip Jeffries wallcovering and a unique mirror design, the solid painted floating cabinet in the powder room became too dominant in the space. By painting it Modern Masters platinum and then glazing it to balance the texture of the grass cloth, the standout elements remained focal and this powder became a jewel in this lovely home.

The den, which is open to the kitchen and breakfast area, features mirror-faced cabinetry flanking the fireplace—a perfect place to hide audio-visual equipment and all the kids' toys and games. Their wooden bead detail was silver leafed, and the full pieces were glazed to create the look of built-in furniture rather than job-built cabinetry. This serves a dual design purpose, balancing the kitchen cabinetry and creating a beautiful visual for the den itself.

RECONFIGURING SPACES

Located in a great neighborhood, with a generous yard, this home had neither the style nor the floorplan that the new owners had envisioned to raise their young family of five. Trusting that a well thought out renovation could transform the home's look and functionality, they took a leap of faith and purchased the house. A first, minor renovation improved the aesthetic and flow. But it was the second, major renovation, years later, that gave these homeowners the stylish functionality they wanted: a dream kitchen and pantry, a mom-central spot, an adult space for quiet visits and a large game room for the kids, all within the structure's original framework.

Wanting to do the design work herself, the homeowner eagerly took my suggestion to hire an architect to help draw her vision. The renovation project began. The couple love natural textures, so reclaimed woods, slurried brick, plastered SegretoStone® counters and lime-based coatings throughout were used. The open metal shelving, enlarged steel-frame window and the plastered ceiling give the kitchen a spacious sense, while the antique fireback and custom metal hood create a focal point over the stove. The result is a dramatic statement room, and exactly what the homeowners wanted.

ARCHITECT *Newberry Architecture* **RENOVATOR** *Parker House Inc.*
PHOTOGRAPHER *Wade Blissard*

Rather than installing brick and painting it white, we decided to plaster over the brick in the same tones as the walls, lending a soft textural effect that paint alone cannot accomplish. When choosing brick to plaster over, any tone will work, but deep ridges or a manufactured repetitive texture may hinder its natural look.

Leslie gave me an incredible tip: to measure everything I wanted to store in my kitchen, butlers, and mom-central before the construction began. It felt like an insane task at the time, but it proved to be invaluable. By customizing the drawer and cabinet sizes to fit what I wanted where, it has helped me to stay organized, feel better equipped, and enjoy my spaces more.

HOMEOWNER

The original mahogany door was stained so dark, it actually looked like it was painted chocolate brown. Instead of replacing it, we stripped, bleached and finished it, enhancing its beautiful carvings and giving it a natural feel.

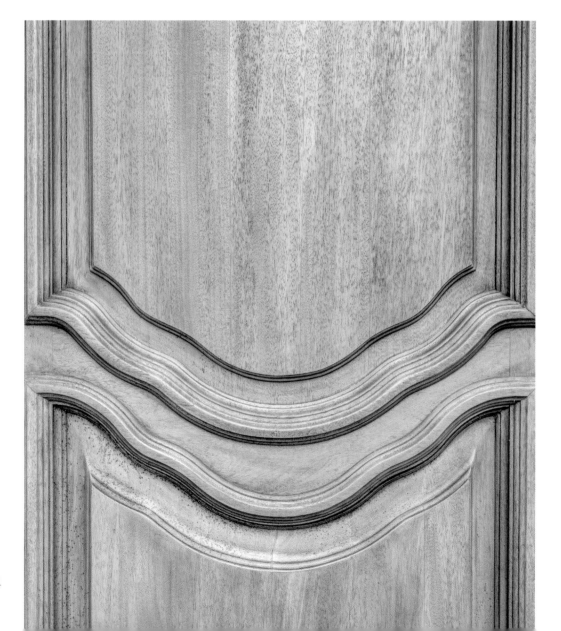

The concept was hatched when I accompanied the clients to see another property they were considering buying. They loved the larger lot, but felt this new house had the same limitation as their current home: a lack of interior function. Coincidently, I knew this prospective home well, having worked on it extensively in the past. Gazing around the two-story living area, I suggested that they drop the ceiling and create a second floor above the space for a game room for the kids. At that moment we looked at each other, all thinking the same thing: This could be done to their existing home, so . . . why move?

If an existing wallcovering has a strong adhesion, the seams can be floated, and the surface primed with an oil-based primer to seal the glue and then painted with a latex paint. In this instance, due to the paper's texture, the seams couldn't be floated. Stenciling an all-over design helped mask the lines of the painted paper.

_____

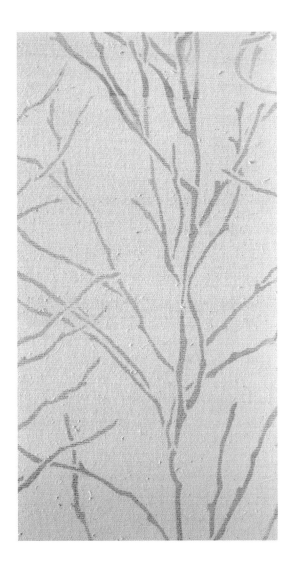

CREATING IMPACT

_____

Having worked on multiple projects with Karyn, I was excited to see her new home. She had already painted it white, replaced the wood front door with an iron one, and refinished the dark wooden floors for a lighter, natural feel. With the light transitional new aesthetic in place, I almost didn't realize I had helped the previous owner fill the home with color and pattern. Karyn wanted to start with the entry and make a plan for the rest of her home. I loved the texture of the white painted over a grasscloth wallcovering but felt we needed to use finishes to give the illusion of a higher ceiling and to create a pop of drama that would balance the décor elements used in connecting rooms. We decided to silver leaf the ceiling and gap in molding, stencil a faint pattern over the grasscloth in silver metallic, and paint a simple yet dramatic graphic on her entry floor. The outcome? A statement entry, which gives you a sense of Karyn's youthful, fun personality, and a feeling you can't wait to see what's to come.

PHOTOGRAPHER *Wade Blissard*

VENETIAN INFUSED WITH GOLD LEAF

CONCRETE WITH GILT OVERLAY

SEGRETOSTONE® BLOCK

WAXED DIAMOND

DIAMOND WITH METAL FOIL OVERLAYS

METALIC BROOMED LIME

VENETIAN

PLASTERS

I fell in love with plaster early in my career, while in search of the right finish for a collaborative design project. The owners wanted their newly built home to feel like they had taken a century-old stone farmhouse and modernized it. I was awarded the contract to "faux finish" the walls. However, I felt there had to be another technique that would better achieve their vision. I couldn't wrap my head around using authentic reclaimed materials for the bones of the home and then unifying the structure with an imitation treatment on the walls and ceilings. After countless hours of research and travels, I discovered the solution—and my enduring passion—right in my backyard. I met Marion Saylors, an old-school plasterer. Together, we began brainstorming how to reinvent the traditional lath and plaster method into a treatment for the sheetrock homes of today. I tinted the finish coat of a historical lime and gypsum plaster, and applied the mix over a properly bonded sheetrock surface. The end product offered a depth and movement I had never before seen. Architecture was enhanced by creating the impression of hand-carved archways and windows that appeared to be set deep within walls. Using plaster allows door, window, crown and base moldings to be minimized while still maintaining the design, thus offsetting the price of the product. Its character truly blends with any surrounding. Thanks to my time with Marion, whom I often call my guardian angel, I have been endlessly captivated by the beauty of natural plaster, which offers a depth and sophistication that has no match.

Designer **CINDY WITMER DESIGNS** *Building Designer* **ROBERT DAME DESIGNS** *Builder* **STONEHENGE CLASSIC HOMES INC.** *Photographer* **LAUREY GLENN**

Designer **TRISHA MCGAW DESIGNS** *Renovator* **PINNACLE CUSTOM BUILDERS** *Photographer* **WADE BLISSARD**

DECORATIVE PAINTING

Decorative painting is a transformative art, creating the illusion that wood is stone or marble, walls are fabric, floors are inlaid wood or tile, or stenciled sheetrock appears as a wallcovering. This artistry can help eyesores like vents and electrical plates to blend in with their surrounding surfaces, allowing the surface beauty to remain uninterrupted. Stenciling has had many evolutions since its first found form in cave paintings dating to 10,000 B.C., where artists sprayed pigment through a hollowed bone around their hands to create a pattern on the walls. Today, thousands of designs are pre-cut and available, allowing for easy customization and an affordable alternative to wall coverings. To further customize, a hand-cut stencil can be formed from a drawing, or, a pattern can be sketched on paper and a tracing wheel used to create tiny holes into the paper. When rubbed with charcoal, dots are left on the wall, creating an outline for a hand-applied repetitive design. The same pattern can look completely different depending on artist application and the level of contrast between your background and stencil color, allowing for a unique interpretation with each application.

TROMPE L'OEIL FABRIC

ALL-OVER STENCIL

TROMPE L'OEIL HORN

ALL-OVER STENCIL

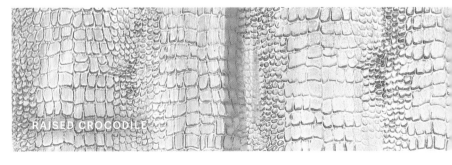

TROMPE L'OEIL MALACHITE

RAISED CROCODILE

ALL-OVER STENCIL

As illustrated by these two fireplace surrounds, many of the treatments we suggest are born from seeking to invent creative, affordable options to mask a surface a homeowner doesn't like, or to create one anew because what the homeowner envisions is nowhere to be found. The top, previously slick black granite was primed, painted, then stenciled to give this fireplace a makeover, allowing it to work in the space. On the bottom surround, designer Jennifer Martinez couldn't find the decorative concrete tile she had in mind to dress this fireplace surround. After limestone was installed instead, we were able to hand draw and paint a pattern that met Jennifer's vision and was original just to her client.

DESIGNER *Jennifer Martinez*
BUILDER *Fairway Companies*
PHOTOGRAPHER *Wade Blissard*

OPPOSITE IMAGE

Many of the repurposed elements in this home were created from beloved antiques from the homeowners' past abodes. The paneling around the fireplace in the formal living room was reworked to fit its new space and reclaimed stone was used on the front façade. The interior brick was new, and felt out of place. Only when the interior firebox was painted to match the exterior old stone did the accent wall became a believable vision of the past.

DESIGNER *Nest & Cot*
PHOTOGRAPHER *Wade Blissard*

When remodeling your home, there are so many ways to
beautifully reinvent pieces that are special to you. A good
carpenter, finisher, and a strong imagination may be all you need.

Designer **CLAUDIA LUMMIS** *Builder* **WINDHAM BUILDERS**
Photographer **WADE BLISSARD**

WOOD

Wood finishes are constantly evolving to keep up with interior design. After centuries of artisans and craftsmen refining their techniques, the possibilities for wood surfaces are truly limitless. Today's finishing trends range from contemporary high-sheen surfaces embellished with metal leafing, to age-old treatments of wire-brushed natural woods. Never before in design have we been so free to mix different period styles, and that flexibility has pushed the decorative arts industry to become equally fresh and diverse in its methods for working with wood. Striving to come up with affordable techniques to reinvent outdated surfaces, such as orange-stained wood, without the expense of stripping and bleaching, we have developed new finishes to give your furnishings, paneling, built-in cabinetry and beams a whole new perspective.

MURALS

Murals are making a big resurgence in the world of interiors, trending on design Instagram feeds across the globe. The finishing touches of your home allow you to personalize your spaces and tell your story, to express who you are and what is beautiful and important to you. Unlike wallpapers, where repeats fall where they may, murals can be scaled to a room without seams. The space's architectural elements, such as windows and doors or groin ceilings, can be easily worked into the design. Rather than having to stop abruptly at the end of a panel, wall or window casement as a wallcovering must, you can curve a mural onto a ceiling or extend a design so it organically falls onto another wall. Curved staircases, domes, niches and any other areas where it's difficult to hang art are perfect places to decorate with murals.

To give a mural a modern interpretation, go large. A simple rose painted 1 to 3 feet in diameter has a totally different feel than one painted to scale. A graphic painted with large shapes will affect your space differently than one with a smaller pattern. Another way to contemporize the mural is to take a traditional subject and paint it in varying tones of the same color. Imagine any of your favorite scenes painted on tones of sepia, taupe, gray or blush. Oversized and bold, or tonal and muted, most murals can be created at a cost savings compared to hand-screened wallcoverings.

Designed by **LESLIE SINCLAIR, KIRBY SINCLAIR**
Mural by **SEGRETO** *Photographer* **WADE BLISSARD**

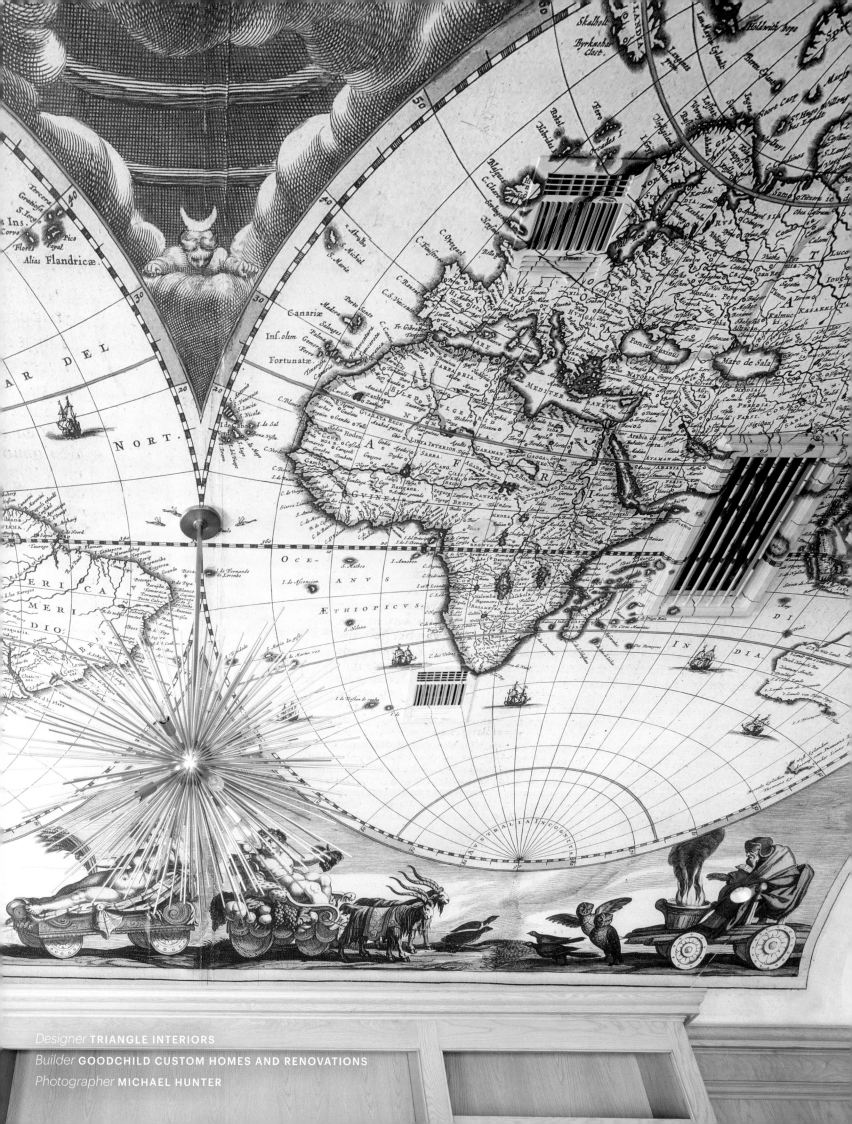

MY FAVORITE GAME OF I SPY

Remember those *I Spy* books we loved to read as kids? I still love playing the game at work. Most of the time we are called upon to enhance people's interiors by creating standout features. But just as important to the aesthetic of a home is the work of disguising elements that distract from its beauty. Light rims, vents, and plates for electrical switches and plugs are huge culprits of visual and aesthetic distraction. By painting them to blend with their surrounding surfaces, the eye no longer is sidetracked by these functional eyesores. We have completed huge projects where we've transformed every surface in the home, and many times it is this masterful painting technique that receives the most attention. Play the game with me and see if you can find these now-hidden elements. I spy...

SOURCES

PARISIAN APARTMENT (PAGES 10-21)

Designer Meg Lonergan. Renovation Architect Tom Wilson & Associates. Renovator Pintail Construction. Photographer Pär Bengtsson. Segreto consultant Leslie Sinclair, assistant Karly Rauch. Plaster throughout by Segreto. SUNROOM: Wood ceiling finish by Segreto. Chandelier from Stephen Antonson. Jean Royere re-edition sofa and chair from M Naeve. Jeanneret chair from 1st Dibs. Floor lamp from Design Within Reach. LIVING ROOM: Plaster shelving by Segreto. Sofa from Flexform. Chairs from Cassina. Leather chair from Kelly Wearstler. Rug from Matt Camron Rugs & Tapestries. Floor lamp and Egg Collective coffee table from M Naeve. STAIRWELL AND POWDER: Venetian plaster by Segreto. Apparatus Studio sconces from M Naeve. Faucet from Fixtures & Fittings. Tile from Ann Sacks. DINING ROOM: Chairs from Gubi. Table from Poltrona Frau. Art between sconces by Paul Rousso and end of table by Roi James from Laura Rathe Fine Art. Sconces from Atelier de Troupe. Chandelier by Lindsey Adelman. Drapery fabric from Schumacher. KITCHEN: Barstools from Holly Hunt. Light from Atelier de Troupe. Kitchen by Eggersmann. Counters from Aria Stone. Shades from Conrad. Faucet from Fixtures & Fittings. MASTER BEDROOM/BATH: Drapery from Schumacher. Sconces and light fixture from Urban Electric. Mirror from BDDW. Hardware and faucet from Waterworks. Sink in his bath from Fixtures & Fittings.

FRENCH MODERN (PAGES 22-35)

Designer Mol. Design. Architect Charles W. Ligon AIA Architects Inc. Builder Kristal Construction. Photographer Wade Blissard. Segreto consultant Leslie Sinclair, assistant Karly Rauch. Plaster and SegretoStone® counters with integrated sinks used throughout by Segreto. 14th–16th c. beams, mantels, reclaimed flooring and all antiques and light fixtures used throughout unless otherwise noted from Renouveau Fine European Antiques. Drapery made by Beatriz Pimentel. Upholstery, custom furniture, headboards and bedding made by Manuel Ruiperez. Florals throughout by Karla Lazo Floral Design. Hardware from Elegant Additions. Trim painted Sherwin Williams Zurich White. DINING ROOM: 19th c. Spanish chairs from Antica Collection. Drapery and cushion fabric from Schumacher. MUSIC ROOM: Black Knoll table from Sunset Settings. Velvet on settee and silk drapery fabric from Schumacher. KITCHEN/ BREAKFAST: Schumacher velvet on antique chairs and bar stools from CB2. Range from Lacanche. ENTRY: Limestone table where Mary is perched custom designed by Mol. Designs. Metal staircase railing by ACI Metal Works. FAMILY ROOM: Custom sofa covered in fabric from ID Collection. Chairs covered in velvet from Schumacher. Coffee table designed by MoL. Design. Fabric on stools and chair from Fortuny. MASTER BEDROOM: 18th c. Portugal altarpiece turned into a headboard from Sheffield Antiques. Drapery and antique chairs fabric from Schumacher. MASTER BATH: Tadelakt shower by Segreto. Sconces from Janet Wiebe. BAR: 18th c. Italian architectural piece from Provenance Antiques.

CLASSIC MODERN (PAGES 36-43)

Designer Slovack-Bass; Marjorie Slovack, RID, ASID, Julie Veselka, ASID, Amy Lopez, RID, and Cali Killian. Renovator CK&H Construction. Photographer Julie Soefer. Segreto consultant Leslie Sinclair, assistant Karly Rauch. ENTRY/SITTING: Layered Venetian plaster by Segreto.

Chandelier from Arteriors. Cocktail table from Sunpan. Console table from Alyson Jon. Rug from Rug Mart Houston. Mirror from LADCO. Lamps from AREA. Drapery fabric from George Cameron Nash by G&S Draperies. Sofa from Mitchell Gold in fabric from Zoffany. STUDY: Layered Venetian Plaster by Segreto. Console from Alyson Jon. Chandelier and writing desk from LADCO. Desk chairs from The Joseph Company in Kravet fabric and ottoman in Pindler fabric. Lounge chairs from Mitchell Gold in Weitzner fabric. Rug from Madison Lily. Gold end table from John Brooks. CLUB: Painting by Kiah Denson from Segreto Gallery. Chandelier from Alyson Jon. Barstools from Arteriors. Rug from Rug Mart Houston. Side tables from West Elm. Chairs from The Joseph Company in Kravet fabric. Ottoman from Alyson Jon. Ceiling wallcovering from Zoffany installed by Rick Krise. GATHERING: Cocktail table top and sofa by The Joseph Company in fabric from Pindler McCoy. Nesting tables, C-table and swivel chairs from Alyson Jon in fabric from Hickory White. Console from Global Views. Ottomans from John Brooks. Rug from Rug Mart Houston. Drapery fabric from Zoffany by G&S Draperies. KITCHEN/DINING: Cabinet finish by Segreto. Backsplash and back painted glass top table from Mirror Gallery with base from Vieux Interiors. Chairs from LADCO in fabric from McCoy Steelcase. Pendants from Mitchell Gold. Counter stools from Mecox.

CONTEMPORARY OASIS (PAGES 44-55)

Designer Trisha McGaw Designs. Building Designer Robert Dame Designs. Builder Allan Edwards Builder Inc. Segreto consultants Leslie Sinclair, Kirby Sinclair. Plaster throughout by Segreto. UPSTAIRS GAME ROOM: Photographer Julie Soefer. Chandelier by Sonneman. Chairs by Ironies. ENTRY: Photographer Wade Blissard. STUDY AND LIVING ROOM: Photographer Julie Soefer. Floors by Custom Floors Unlimited. Desk from Vieux Interiors. Chair and occasional table from Design House. Sculptures from David Sutherland. SegretoStone® fireplace wall by Segreto. Flooring from Alamo Stone. Sofa from Tomlinson. Chairs from Internum. DINING ROOM: Photographer dining room Wade Blissard, exterior Julie Soefer. Beam finish by Segreto. Custom table designed by Trisha McGaw, fabricated by James Dawson Design, Inc. Custom chairs by Custom Creations Furniture. Custom light fixture by Sonneman. KITCHEN/BAR: Photographer Julie Soefer. Beam, cabinet finishes and SegretoStone® bar top by Segreto. Wood kitchen island and bar countertop by Custom Floors Unlimited. Light fixtures from Currey and Company. Custom vent hood by Lonestar Range Hood Co. Bench and artwork from Design House. MASTER BED/SITTING: Photography by Wade Blissard. Rug from Creative Flooring. Bed by Bernhardt Furniture Company. Bedding from Kuhl-Linscomb. MASTER BATH/CLOSET: Photography by Julie Soefer. Plaster and cabinet finishes by Segreto. Tile flooring from Daltile.

IT'S ALL IN THE MIX (PAGES 56-61)

Designer Wren Design; Amy Murchison. Renovator UrbanCraft Custom Builders, LP. Photographer Wade Blissard. Segreto consultant Andrea Condara. Waxed plaster throughout by Segreto. LIVING ROOM: Painting by Ashley Longshore. Resin bowl from Mecox. Antique tiger striped fauteuil chair and Italian consoles and black lamps from Shabby Slips. Sofas from Boxwood Interiors. Pillows covered in Casamance fabric and draperies by Heine's Custom Draperies.

Hide and metal chairs from Lam Bespoke. Lime green stools from Mecox. Spanish trestle table from Joyce Horn Antiques. Rug and art by Edgar Podzemny from Madison Lily. Art prints by Victor Vasarely from Skelton Culver. DINING ROOM: Mirror finish by Segreto. Chairs and art from Vieux Interiors. Black oval Saarinen table from Design Within Reach. Rug from Madison Lily. ENTRY: Chandelier by Andy Coolquitt from Winston Contemporary Art. Rug from Matt Camron Rugs & Tapestries. Acrylic art from FOUND. Green settee from W. Gardner, Ltd. Mirror and antique chest from AREA.

SERENITY IN TRANSITION (PAGES 62–69)

Designer JJ Designs. Building Designer Rice Residential Design, L.L.C. Builder Goodchild Custom Homes and Renovations. Photographer Wade Blissard. Segreto consultant Leslie Sinclair. Plaster throughout by Segreto. ENTRY: Staircase runner from STARK. Antique chairs from MAI Memorial Antiques & Interiors. KITCHEN: Cabinet finishes by Segreto. Bar stools by Creative Style Furniture covered in Cowtan &Tout fabric. Hardware from Morrison Supply Company. Flooring from Pomo+ADR. DINING ROOM: China cabinet and dining chairs from Joyce Horn Antiques. Drapery velvet from Scalamandre, trimmed in Samuel & Sons. Sisal rug by STARK. MASTER RETREAT: Cabinet finishes by Segreto. Trumeau mirror, sconces and chests from Joyce Horn Antiques. White marble countertops from Omni. Honed marble tile from Pomo+ADR. Drapery fabric by Clarke & Clarke. Custom headboard covered in fabric from Colefax and Fowler. Custom bedding by JJ Design Group. Chandelier from Janet Wiebe. Bench covered in fabric from Cowtan &Tout. Custom chairs by Creative Style Furniture in fabric from Duralee.

SPANISH REVIVAL (PAGES 70–83)

Architectural Consultant and Designer Sarah West & Associates. Renovator Parker House, Inc. Photographer Pär Bengtsson. Segreto consultants Leslie Sinclair, Kirby Sinclair. Plaster throughout by Segreto. LIVING ROOM: Ombre Velvet chairs from Casa Italia. Larchmont chairs from Kelly Wearstler. Sofa from Kravet. Rug from Kyle Bunting. Stools from AREA. Hanging fixture and coffee table from Round Top Antiques Fair. ENTRY: Chandelier from Provenance Antiques. Bench from Back Row Home. Sconces from Solaria Lighting. LIBRARY: SegretoStone® shelves by Segreto. Ivory Cowhide Rug from David Alan Rugs. Suede for Antique Chairs from Tandy Leather. KITCHEN/KEEPING ROOM: SegretoStone® hood and Spanish texture for fireplace by Segreto. Bar Stools from Holly Hunt. Fireplace screen from Moxie. Rug from Kravet. POWDERS: Plastered planking and SegretoStone® sink by Segreto. Antique sink and flooring from Chateau Dominque. MASTER BED/ BATH: Plastered finish on tile by Segreto. 18th c. bench from Back Row Home. Headboard from W. Gardner, Ltd. Antique tile for fireplace and flooring in master bath from Chateau Dominque. Rug from Creative Flooring. Chair from Susan Horne Antiques. Accessories in bath from Laurier Blanc. MASTER CLOSET: Chaise from Shabby Slips.

CALMING RETREAT (PAGES 84–91)

Designer The Owen Group Design Firm; Tami Owen, Brelan Owen. Builder Lisenby Co Inc. Architect Architectural Solutions, Inc. Photographer Wade Blissard. Segreto consultant Kirby Sinclair. Plaster throughout by Segreto. Art consultant Bailey Miller with Dimmitt Contemporary Art. Floors from Doro's Unique Flooring. Trim color Benjamin Moore White Dove. ENTRY: Lighting from Brown. Table and accessories from Shabby Slips. COCKTAIL ROOM: Swivel chairs and chandelier from AREA. Coffee table from Shabby Slips. Custom made lamps by Rachel Alcock. Drapery in Kravet fabric, with trim from Holly Hunt, by Horton Draperies. Custom rug from Creative Flooring. LIVING ROOM: Custom velvet sofa, slip covered chairs, custom pillows and accessories from Shabby Slips. Rug from Creative Flooring. Custom coffee table by James Dawson Design, Inc. KITCHEN/BREAKFAST: Chairs by Lee Industries from John Brooks Showroom. Light fixtures from Brown. Concrete table from Mecox.

SPANISH COLONIAL (PAGES 92–101)

Designer Garrett Hunter. Architect Michael Landrum. Builder Morris Hullinger. Photographer Pär Bengtsson. Segreto consultants Leslie Sinclair, Leslie Simmons. Plaster throughout by Segreto. ENTRY: Painting by Julian Schnabel. Stone sculpture by Pedro Coronel. Bronze torso by Aristide Maillol. Stone and iron table by Balinskas Imports. LIVING ROOM: Resin chair by Olivier Gregoire. Pair of chairs by Pierre Jeanneret. Steel cocktail table, Mexican Tonola vase, various stone and wood sculptures and art deco Chinese screens from Tienda X Gallery. Lips sofa by Charles James. KITCHEN: Kitchen mural by Jaime Loera. Lamp by Christopher Kreiling from Tienda X Gallery. DOWNSTAIRS GALLERY: Venetian tête-à-tête from Tiendra X Gallery. Painting by Rosson Crow from The Hole Gallery. DINING ROOM: Chairs by Poul Kjaerholm. Antique Oaxaca dining table from Tienda X Gallery. Painting by Robert de Niro, Sr. UPSTAIRS GALLERY: Pair of 17th c. Italian chairs from the estate of William Randolph Hearst. Syrian 19th c. tabouret from Tienda X Gallery. 19th c. silk Kirman rug from Persia.

COUNTRY FRENCH (PAGES 102–111)

Designer Lucas/Eilers Design Associates L.L.P.; Sarah Eilers, Laura Beth Rickway. Architect Architectural Solutions, Inc. Builder Abercrombie Custom Homes, L.P. Segreto consultant Leslie Sinclair. Plaster and cabinet finish throughout by Segreto. ENTRY: Photographer Wade Blissard. Sconces from Brown. Reclaimed limestone floors from Chateau Dominque. LIVING ROOM: Photographer Wade Blissard. Rug from Matt Camron Rugs & Tapestries. Chandelier from Bill Gardner Antiques. Art from Gremillion & Co. Fine Art, Inc. Lounge chairs from Brunschwig & Fils, Inc. Antique mantel from Chateau Dominque. DINING ROOM: Photographer Wade Blissard. Art from Gremillion & Co. Fine Art, Inc. Rug from Matt Camron Rugs & Tapestries. Chandelier from Skelton & Culver Antiques and Interiors. KITCHEN/BREAKFAST: Photographer Wade Blissard. Cabinets painted Sherwin Williams Useful Gray then finished by Segreto. Antique cement tile from Chateau Dominque. Stone counters from Vivaldi Stone. Hood from Materials Marketing. Barstools from Sterling. MASTER BEDROOM/ BATH: Photographer Julie Soefer. Bath cabinets painted Sherwin Williams Gray Clouds then finished by Segreto. Art from Dimmitt Contemporary Art. Bed custom designed by Sarah Eilers. Bedding from Leontine Linens. Chandelier from Joyce Horn Antiques. Rug from Matt Cameron Rugs & Tapestries. Sectional from A. Rudin. Tufted Ottoman from Vanguard. Counters from Vivaldi Stone. Tile from Walker Zanger. Mirrors from Janet Wiebe. Sconces from Circa Lighting. Vanity chair from George Cameron Nash.

CLASSIC EUROPEAN (PAGES 112–123)

Designer Ohara Davies-Gaetano Interiors. Photographer Wade Blissard. Segreto consultant Leslie Sinclair. Plaster and cabinet finish throughout by Segreto. Flooring throughout by Custom Floors Unlimited. Mantels and antiques sourced in Europe by Ohara Davis-Gaetano Interiors unless noted. DEN: Reclaimed doors going into bar from Chateau Dominque. Custom sofas in fabric by Kravet. Lighting made by artisans in France out of salvaged wood. 18th c. Gustavian ottomans covered in Rogers & Goffigon fabric. LIVING ROOM: Mirrors flanking mantel from Thompson + Hanson, finish tweaked by Segreto. Chandeliers by David Iatesta from Nicky Rising. DINING ROOM: Chandelier by David Iatesta from Nicky Rising. Client's chairs covered in Perennials fabric. Custom host chairs covered in fabric by Mark Alexander. Drapery fabric by Rogers & Goffigon. KITCHEN: Hood designed by Ohara Davis-Gaetano Interiors and finished by Segreto. Roche limestone counters, custom glazed white Moroccan tile backsplash and limestone flooring from Concept Studio. MASTER SUITE: Reclaimed doors throughout from Chateau Domingue. Pond at Castle Planegg painting by Otto Pippel c. 1920. STUDY: 19th c. French mantel, added to by renovator and finished by Segreto. Rug from Caravan. Chandeliers by David Iatesta from Nicky Rising.

SOFT MODERN (PAGES 124–129)

Designer and Photographer Benjamin Johnston. Architect John Wawrose. Builder Brookstone Homes. Segreto consultant Kirby Sinclair. DINING ROOM/BAR: Venetian Plaster by Segreto. Oval Onyx Bowl by Ron Dier Design. Bronze totem by Corbin Bronze, entitled "Evolution." Artwork by Stallman Studio from Laura Rathe Fine Art. Bench by Custom Creations. Dining chairs from Interlude Home. LIVING ROOM: Rug from Madison Lily. Kravet sofa with fabric by Peter Dunham. Chairs from Thayer Coggin. Shagreen side table from Made Goods. Twine stools from Palecek. Desk from Sonder Living. MASTER BEDROOM: Plaster by Segreto. Painting by Audra Weaser from Laura Rathe Fine Art. Rug from Madison Lily. Bedding from Plush Home and Restoration Hardware. Lounge chairs by Kravet. Vintage stool from Lynn Goode Vintage Furniture + Decorative Arts. Reading lamps by Circa Lighting.

FORMAL FRENCH COUNTRY (PAGES 130–137)

Designer Trisha McGaw Designs. Building Designer Robert Dame Designs. Builder Allan Edwards Builder Inc. Photographer Wade Blissard. Segreto consultants Leslie Sinclair, Kirby Sinclair. MUD/WINE ROOM: Monograms on lockers and mural by Segreto. Flooring from Materials Marketing. Lighting from Lighting Inc. POWDER: Stencil over plaster by Segreto. Chest from Joyce Horn Antiques. Mirror from MAI Memorial Antiques & Interiors. Sconces from Lighting Inc. Sink from Hollywood Builders Hardware. FAMILY ROOM/KITCHEN: Glazed cabinetry by Segreto. Custom upholstered goods from Lam Bespoke and Custom Creations. Rugs from Madison Lily. Art over mantel by Kelly Morley. Chandeliers from Lighting Inc. MASTER BEDROOM/BATH: Waxed plaster and cabinet glazing by Segreto. Headboard by Custom Creations. Rug from Madison Lily. Bedding from Kuhl-Linscomb. Chandeliers from Lighting Inc. Flooring from Materials Marketing. Tub and fixtures from Hollywood Builders Hardware.

FRENCH WHIMSY (PAGES 138–145)

Designer Dodson Interiors. Builder Elron Construction. Photographer Julie Soefer. Segreto consultant Leslie Sinclair. STUDY: Cerused paneling by Segreto. Chandelier from Arteriors. Sisal rug from Creative Flooring. Decorative rug from Matt Camron Rugs & Tapestries. Palm tree from FOUND. Bench from MAI Memorial Antiques & Interiors. DINING ROOM: Chandelier from Skelton Culver. Art Barbara Davis Gallery. Rug from Matt Camron Rugs &Tapestries. Custom chairs designed by Julie Dodson and made by The Joseph Company. Table from George Cameron Nash. BUTLERS: Back splash from Pomo+ADR. Hardware from Morrison Supply Company. KITCHEN: Cabinet and beam finish by Segreto. Pitch forks from MAI Memorial Antiques & Interiors. Custom barstools by The Joseph Company. Light fixtures from Aidan Gray. Custom hood by Elron Construction. BREAKFAST ROOM: Beam finish by Segreto. Metal remnants from Carl Moore Home. Table and chairs from M Naeve. Reclaimed doors from Round Top Antiques Fair. Antique piece from Liz Spradling Antiques. Chandelier from Circa Lighting. LIVING ROOM: Stools, velvet chairs in Osborne & Little fabric and custom sofa covered in Twill Sugar from

Link Outdoor by The Joseph Company. Metal consoles, art above and dog from MAI Memorial Antiques & Interiors. Art above mantel from Barbara Davis Gallery. Coffee table from FOUND. MASTER BEDROOM: Settee and chests from Joyce Horn Antiques. Rug from Rug Mart. Mirrors and lamps from Reid's Antiques. Custom headboard made by The Joseph Company. Bedding from Plush Home. MATER BATH: Reclaimed doors from Round Top Fair Antiques Fair. Decorative tile from Pomo+ADR. Tub and fixtures from Morrison Supply Company. Chest from MAI Memorial Antiques & Interiors. Art Work from David Shelton Gallery. Rug from Matt Camron Rugs & Tapestries.

SENSATIONAL SHOWCASE (PAGES 146–153)

Designer Elizabeth Garrett Interiors. Architect Architectural Solutions, Inc. Builder Cupic Custom Homes. Segreto Consultant Kirby Sinclair. LIVING ROOM: Photographer Wade Blissard. Plaster by Segreto. Antique mantel from Materials Marketing. Reclaimed wood flooring by Doro's Unique Flooring. Lighting from Visual Comfort. ENTRY: Photographer Felix Sanchez. Plaster by Segreto. Art by Zhuang Hong Yi from Laura Rathe Fine Art. Italian stone from Ann Sacks inlaid into reclaimed wood by Doro's Unique Wood Flooring. KITCHEN: Photographers Kerry Kirk and Wade Blissard. Cabinet Finish and SegretoStone® island top by Segreto. Cabinets by McCaw Cabinetry. Pendants from Visual Comfort. Reclaimed beams from Woodshop of Texas. Range from ILVE. Custom hood by Cupic Custom Homes. Custom barstools by Talbot Cooley. BAR: Photographer Wade Blissard. Gold leaf bead detail by Segreto. Cielo polished quartzite counters from Pomo+ADR. Davlin Rose Gold mirrored backsplash tiles from Ann Sacks. DINING ROOM: Designer for furnishings Talbot Cooley. Photographer Kerry Kirk. Waxed plaster by Segreto. Rug from Madison Lily. Chairs from Lorin Marsh. Table from Julian Chichester. POWDER BATH: Photographer Wade Blissard. Wall and cabinet finishes by Segreto.

ETHEREAL ELEGANCE (PAGES 154–163)

Designer The Owen Group Design Firm; Tami Owen, Brelan Owen. Architect Architectural Soulutions, Inc. Builder Goodchild Custom Homes and Renovations, Scott Sorba. Photographer Wade Blissard. Segreto consultant Kirby Sinclair. Plaster thoughout by Segreto. Art consultant Bailey Miller with Dimmitt Contemporary Art. Limestone flooring from Alamo Stone. DINING ROOM: Flooring by Custom Floors Unlimited. Silk drapery fabric by Great Plains. Custom hide rug from Creative Flooring. Selenite chandelier by Ron Dier from David Sutherland. Custom dining table top by James Dawson Design, Inc. on zinc base. Painting by Mallory Page. Buffet, lamps and accessories from Shabby Slips. Custom-made dining chairs covered in fabric from Holly Hunt. LIVING ROOM: Custom upholstery by Custom Creations, sofa fabric by Perennials, arm chair fabric by Larsen. Coffee table and lamp from AREA. Art by Mallory Page. Lanterns from Brown. Drapery hardware from Peck & Company, fabric from Holly Hunt. ENTRY: Doors and shutters from Atelier Domingue. Montecito Lantern by Formations from Culp Associates. Doors into bar from Chateau Domingue. KITCHEN: Lanterns from Visual Comforts. Calacatta honed counters and backsplash from Omni Stone. POWDER: Waxed plaster by Segreto. Hand blown sconces from Holly Hunt. Mirror from AREA. Antique glass wall from Dauphin Sales. Lorford Smoke Bell Lantern from Visual Comfort & Co. Steel door and window from Atelier Domingue. MASTER: Bedding from Kuhl-Linscomb. Chandelier and drapery from Holly Hunt with trim from Schumacher. Rug from Creative Flooring. Bench from AREA.

VINTAGE GLAM (PAGES 164–173)

Architectural Consultant and Designer Sarah West & Associates. Photographer Wade Blissard, Pär Bengtsson. Plaster throughout by

Segreto. Segreto consultants Leslie Sinclair, Kirby Sinclair. LIVING ROOM: Fireplace mantel from Chateau Domingue. Vintage white ottoman from Back Row Home recovered in fabric from Holly Hunt. Chairs from Round Top Antique Show, lacquered black and covered in long haired white cowhide. Bar cart side table from Laurier Blanc. Vintage sheepskin chair from Forsyth. Antique enfilade and brass coffee table from Janet Wiebe. Art from Reeves Fine Art. Driftwood side table from Paul Michael Company. Mohair chaise lounges designed by Sarah West. DINING ROOM: 18th c. Buffet Deaux Corps from Chateau Domingue. Chairs from Antica Collection. Belgian champagne bucket from Laurier Blanc. Antique Linen press used as dining table from Marche Paul Bert. Swan from Round Top Antique Show. Mirrors from Shabby Slips. Custom designed lounge by Sarah West. KITCHEN: Antique Island from Marche Paul Bert. Murano vases from Back Row Home. Brass backsplash from Peck & Company. Range by Lacanche. Brass Stools from CB2. PANTRY: Marble from IGM. Art from Round Top Antique Show. FOYER: Tessellated marble console from Moxie. Art by Mike Kirby. BAR: Mirror from Mecox. POWDER ROOM: Fixtures from Hollywood Builders Hardware.

MEDITERRANEAN REVIVAL (PAGES 174–183)

Designer JJ Designs; Kathy and Heather Johnson. Original Architect Francis Burrall Hoffman. Renovation Architect Ray Fenton. Builder Ball Construction. Building Consultant Goodchild Custom Homes and Renovations. Photographer Jean Allsopp. Segreto Consultant Leslie Sinclair. Plaster and wood finishing throughout by Segreto. Floor refinishing by Custom Floors Unlimited. Tile from Pomo+ADR.

TIMELESS MEDITERRANEAN (PAGES 184–193)

Designer Kara Childress, Inc. Photographer Wade Blissard. Segreto Consultants Leslie Sinclair, Kirby Sinclair. Plaster throughout by Segreto. ENTRY: Custom library doors by The Joseph Company. STUDY/DINING: Vents and cans painted to match ceiling wallcovering by Segreto. Chandelier from Lindsey Adelman. Chairs from Verellen. Antique balcony topped with Chamaret stone from Chateau Domingue. Mirror from Kelly Wearstler. GREAT ROOM: Daybed and sofa upholstery in mohair & leather and custom pillows in Holland & Sherry fabric by The Joseph Company. Chest and ottoman from Formations. Rug from Creative Flooring. Antique journals on mantel from Joyce Horn Antiques. KITCHEN/PANTRY: Doors finished to feel reclaimed and glazed kitchen cabinetry by Segreto. Reclaimed Belgian bluestone counters from Chateau Domingue. Chandelier from Formations. Custom barstools from Neal & Company Upholstery. POWDER/DEN: Concrete tile from Chateau Domingue. Custom blackout draperies from Heine's Custom Draperies. Linen sectional from Lee Industries. Custom cerused oak coffee table by Zac Elkins. Rug from Creative Flooring.

MODERN YORKSHIRE COUNTRYSIDE (PAGES 194–201)

Designer, Furnishings Allyson Tracy Plummer. Designer, Hard surfaces Tracy Design Studio. Builder Montecito Builders. Photographer Wade Blissard. Segreto Consultants Leslie Sinclair, Leslie Simmons. Plaster throughout by Segreto. LIVING ROOM: Art by Kevin Gillentine from Laura Rathe Fine Art. Custom chairs by Custom Creations. Rug from Madison Lily. DINING ROOM: Rug from Madison Lily.

STATELY ELEGANCE (PAGES 202–207)

Designer Chandos Interiors. Builder Goodchild Custom Homes and Renovations, John Goodchild. Photographer Laurey Glenn. Segreto Consultant Kirby Sinclair. Plaster throughout by Segreto. Upholstery work by The Joseph Company. Shades and drapery custom made by

D & D Drapery. FAMILY ROOM: Custom sofas in fabric by Great Plains. Washington lounger brass chair frame from Artistic Frame covered in Comet, Graphite fabric from Great Plains. Pair shagreen commodes from R&Y Augousti. Vintage Italian mirrors over chest from Jean-Marc Fray. Murano standing lamp from Kirby Antiques. Antique rug from Retorra. LIVING ROOM: French 1930's curved back chairs from BK Antiques covered in Fortuny Favo Blue and Gold fabric from Wells Abbott Showroom. Galaxy side tables and bench stools by R&Y Agousti from AREA. Custom fireplace screens by Peck & Company. DINING ROOM: Marcel table from Quintus. Chairs from Baker Furniture in Oden Navy fabric from Holland and Sherry. Antique Louis XVI buffet from Jean-Marc Fray. Drapery panels with embroidery by Holland & Sherry. MASTER BEDROOM: Custom bed by The Joseph Company. Bedside chests from George Cameron Nash. Dresser by Quintus from Culp Associates. Bedding from Plush Home. Rug from Rug Mart Houston. Lamps by Daniel Barney from Objets Plus Inc.

FRENCH ACADIAN (PAGES 208–217)

Designer Lucas/Eilers Design Associates L.L.P.; Sarah Eilers. Architect Craig Stiteler Design. Builder K&C Classic Homes. Photographer Julie Soefer. Segreto Consultant Leslie Sinclair. DINING ROOM: Plaster by Segreto. Art by Joseph Adolphe from Gremillion & Co. Fine Art. 19th c. bistro bench from Provenance Antiques in fabric from Cowtan & Tout. Antique chandelier from Tucker Payne Antiques. Oushak rug from Matt Camron Rugs & Tapestries. Antique dining table from E.C. Dicken, Inc. Custom Belgrave side chairs from Woodland Furniture LLC. covered in Colefax & Fowler "Carlow" fabric. Kerry Joyce "Turandot" in Sea Spray drapery fabric from George Cameron Nash. Directoire style antique mirror from Joyce Horn Antiques. KITCHEN/BREAKFAST: Cabinet finishes by Segreto. Taj Mahal honed counters from Design Stone Center. Rangehood, Duquesa Alba Mezzanote Deco tile and custom Duquesa Crimini field tile from Walker Zanger. Barstools from Hickory Chair. Custom lanterns from Brown. Antique table from Back Row Home. Panache Designs barley twist chairs from ID Collection covered in Lee Jofa "Montaigne" and Great Plains "Masquerade" from Holly Hunt. Vassaro Round Chandelier from Culp Associates. Shadow Box Frame from Vestige. Seljuk rug from Matt Camron Rugs & Tapestries. FAMILY ROOM: Hickory Chair sofa covered in Lee Jofa "Sweet Grass" in beige. Formations Tavolino coffee table from Culp Associates. Tabriz Rug from Matt Camron Rugs & Tapestries. Charles Rush lounge chair and ottoman from ID Collection covered in Kerry Joyce "Simone" in lake blue. STUDY: Plaster by Segreto. Sofa from A. Rudin covered in Hodsoll McKenzie "Dover Linen Velvet" from George Cameron Nash. Paul Ferrante Madison Coffee Table from George Cameron Nash. Oushak Rug from Matt Camron Rugs & Tapestries. Theodore Alexander "Verena" Lounge Chair from Bunch & Shoemaker covered in Colefax and Fowler fabric from Culp Associates. Antique chandelier from Brown. POWDER BATH: Plaster by Segreto. Antique Italian sconces from The Gray Door. Counter top from ICM Marble & Granite. 19th c. commode from Art & Antique Hunter. Antique marble sink from Pittet Architecturals. Mirror from Joyce Horn Antiques. BUNKBED ROOM: U-shaped, slipcovered sectional from Lee Industries. Indoor/Outdoor rug from Dash & Albert. Antique table and bench from Janet Wiebe. MASTER BEDROOM/SITTING: Plaster by Segreto. Trim painted Sherwin Williams Extra White. Bedframe from Ebanista. Shapeero rug from STARK. Nightstands from Bernhardt Furniture. Lamps on nightstands from David Sutherland. Leslie Parke Prints from Gremillion & Co. Fine Art. Swivel lounge chairs from A. Rudin covered in Zoffany "Hibano" in Honeycomb. Custom Round Tufted Ottoman from Lozano Upholstery. Bench from Formations. MASTER BATHROOM: Plaster by Segreto. Garden stool from Mecox Gardens. Wall sconces from Joyce Horn Antiques.

Designer **TRIANGLE INTERIORS** Photographer **KERRY KIRK**

Architecture and Design NEWBERRY ARCHITECTURE
Builder GOODCHILD CUSTOM HOMES AND RENOVATIONS
Photographer LAUREY GLENN

A TUSCAN VIBE (PAGES 218–225)

Designer Triangle Interiors; Nicole Zarr. Building Designer Colby Design. Builder Goodchild Custom Homes and Renovations, Scott Burns, Brad Burns. Segreto Consultant Leslie Sinclair. Plaster and cabinet finish throughout by Segreto. Flooring throughout by Custom Floors Unlimited. GREAT ROOM: Photographer Ray Perez. Custom sofas with Brunschwig & Fils fabric. Club chairs from Schumacher. Vintage mirrored floor lamps from AREA. PANTRY: Photographer Wade Blissard. KITCHEN: Photographer Ray Perez. HER OFFICE: Photography by Michael Hunter. Floor design by Segreto. Grass cloth wallcovering from Phillip Jeffries. MASTER SUITE: Photographer Michael Hunter. Beam finishes by Segreto. Drapery Fabric from Cowtan & Tout. Tub and fixtures from Fixtures and Fittings. Tile from POMO+ADR.

HISTORY REINTERPRETED (PAGES 226–243)

Architectural Consultant and Designer Sarah West & Associates. Building Designer Robert Dame Designs. Builder Parker House Inc. Photographer Wade Blissard. Segreto Consultants Leslie Sinclair, Kirby Sinclair. Plaster throughout by Segreto. Wood floors by Doro's Unique Flooring. Steel windows and doors from Atelier Domingue. Landscaping, Oasis Landscape Architects. ENTRY: Staircase railing and settee finished by Segreto. 18th c. altar from a private chapel in the Touraine region of France and 17th c. stone wine room surround from a country bastide near Lyon from Chateau Domingue. Sconces from Skelton Culver Antiques. STUDY: 18th c. cheminee from a Domaine in the Macon region of France from Chateau Domingue. Chandelier from Joyce Horn Antiques. GREAT ROOM: Painting over mantel by Page Gregory Matthews. Daybed in Holly Hunt Fabric, sofa and swivel chair fabric from Pindler, from Lam Bespoke. Rug from Turkish Carpets. Light fixtures from Back Row Home. 18th c. stone cheminee from a farm in the Lorraine Region of France, antique firebrick and reclaimed doors from Chateau Domingue. Salvaged architectural glass perched on brass bases to form a coffee table designed by Sarah West. KITCHEN: Back cabinetry finish and plaster range hood by Segreto. 17th c. French Sacriste cabinet serving as island from Chateau Domingue. Hanging lanterns from a castle in Monferrato, Italy from Antica Collection. Range by Lacanche. DINING ROOM: Barnacle-covered urn from AREA. Italian chandelier and Swedish Rococo table from Antica Collection, with marble slab added. Fabric on dining seats from Pindler, with hand-screened back fabric by Michael Devine. 18th c. French Volet doors integrated into plaster walls from Chateau Domingue. MASTER BEDROOM: French antique bookcase from Round Top Antique Fair. Vintage European brass coffee table from Back Row Home. Italian vintage Murano chandelier from Brown. Sofa covered in fabric by Holly Hunt. MASTER BATH: Cabinet, shutter and wrought iron finishes by Segreto. Chandelier from Currey and Co. Silk Portfolio soaking tub from Hollywood Builders Hardware. Vanity Mirrors from Shabby Slips.

BEAUTIFULLY ECLECTIC (PAGES 244–255)

Architecture and Design Newberry Architecture; Clint Johnson, Gina Brown, Elizabeth Echols. Builder Goodchild Custom Homes and Renovations, Brad Burns. Photographer Laurey Glenn. Segreto Consultant Kirby Sinclair. Plaster throughout by Segreto. Wood flooring from Custom Floors Unlimited. Steel windows from Atelier Domingue. Custom Drapery by D & D Drapery. ENTRY: SegretoStone® hearth by Segreto. Wallcovering from Elitis. DINING: Wallcovering from STARK. Leather chandelier from Ngala Trading Company. FAMILY ROOM: Light fixture from Bone Simple. Painting by Ashley Longshore. KITCHEN: Finish on hood by Segreto. Island shelving by James Dawson Design, Inc. Light fixtures from Urban Electric. Hardware from Holland & Sherry. Tile on hood wall from Ann Sacks. Barstools from Ochre.

BREAKFAST ROOM/EXTERIOR: SegretoStone® fireplace by Segreto. Light fixture from Bone Simple. Custom banquette and chairs by The Joseph Company. Table bases from Julian Chichester. White chair from JANUS et Cie. Side chair and table from KETTAL. MASTER BATH: Custom mirrors by James Dawson Design, Inc. Thassos marble inlaid floors from Pomo+ADR. Plumbing from Hollywood Builders Hardware.

A BIT OF SHIMMER (PAGES 258–267)

Designer Trisha McGaw Designs. Builder Pinnacle Custom Builders. Photographer Wade Blissard. Segreto consultants Leslie Sinclair, Kirby Sinclair. Wall and trim color throughout Sherwin Williams Crushed Ice. ENTRY: Fontaine Chandeliers by Eloquence. Console table from Neiman Marcus. Custom upholstered bench by Trisha McGaw. DINING ROOM: SegretoStone® fireplace surround and plaster by Segreto. Demilunes and dining table from Joyce Horn Antiques. Painting by Debbie Moseley. Chandelier from Lighting Treasures. Mirrors behind sconces from Aidan Gray. Rug from Creative Flooring. CLUB ROOM/BAR: Plaster and limewash by Segreto. Rug from Madison Lily. Antique chandelier from Janet Wiebe. Cocktail table from Arteriors. Swivel chairs from Ashland. Taj Mahal quartzite counters and Tangent Zephyr Calcutta backsplash from Walker Zanger. Bar cabinetry painted Sherwin Williams Agreeable Grey. KITCHEN: Island and pantry door painted Sherwin Williams Grey Matters then finished by Segreto. Plaster hood by Segreto. Kitchen perimeter cabinets painted Sherwin Williams Eider White. Perla Venata leathered quartzite counters and Tuileries Blanc Arabesque backsplash from Walker Zanger. Anise Chandelier from Currey and Company. FAMILY ROOM: Custom SegretoStone® cube table and art piece by Segreto. Chandelier from Lighting Treasures. Acrylic coffee table and Bristol chairs from Lam Bespoke.

UPDATED CLASSIC (PAGES 268–279)

Designer Ellie Bale. Architect Joshua I.F. Jones. Builder Goodchild Custom Homes and Renovations, Juan Hernandez, Adam Hernandez. Photographer Wade Blissard. Segreto Consultants Leslie Sinclair, Kirby Sinclair. FAMILY ROOM/BAR: Cabinets, design on step and barstool refinishing by Segreto covered in fabric by Bunny Williams. Custom sofa and chairs upholstered in a cotton velvet from Lee Jofa. Bench from AREA upholstered in fabric by David Hicks from Lee Jofa. Coffee table from FOUND. Rug from Turkish Carpets. Lamps from Lam Bespoke. Photograph by Miwa Nishimura. Cake art by Gary Komarin. Custom chandelier by Murano. EXTERIOR: Light fixtures from Circa Lighting. Landscape by Oasis Landscape Architects. POWDER BATH: Plaster and finish on Swedish chest by Segreto. Sconces by The Urban Electric Co. Mirror from Joyce Horn Antiques. Fixtures from Lighting Inc. ENTRY: Plaster, SegretoStone® tops and refinished bases to two antique consoles by Segreto. Rug from Turkish Carpets. Chandelier from AREA. Chair from MAI Memorial Antiques & Interiors. STUDY: Plaster ceiling and paneling finish by Segreto. Eames chair and ottoman from Herman Miller. Drapery and bench fabric from Schumacher. Art from Gremillion Gallery. Lamps and side tables from Wendow. DINING ROOM/BUTLERS: Plaster finish by Segreto. Cabinetry painted Sherwin Williams Cloudburst and finished by Segreto. Hardware from Lighting Inc. Sideboard from Joyce Horn Antiques. Linen velvet chair fabric from Kravet. Table from Carl Moore Antiques. Oushak rug from Turkish Carpets. Mirror from Back Row Antiques. Sconces from Marburger Farms Antique Show. Drapery fabric by Miles Red. Artwork by Gary Komarin. KITCHEN: Appliances from Wolf and Sub-Zero. Pendants from Circa Lighting. Custom hood designed by Ellie Bale and fabricated by builder. Hardware from Lighting Inc. CHINA CLOSET: Sherwin Williams Reflecting Pool high gloss.

Photographer WADE BLISSARD

CLASSICISM MEETS MODERNISM (PAGES 280–287)

Designer Don Connelly. Original Architect Aynesworth. Renovation Building Designer Colby Design. Renovator Kerr Construction LLC. Photography by Wade Blissard. Segreto Consultants Leslie Sinclair, Kirby Sinclair. CIGAR FOYER: Venetian Plaster by Segreto. Chandelier from Baccarat. Front doors by Patina Metals. Flooring from Pomo+ADR. Drapery fabric from SAHCO. ENTRY: Staircase runner from Creative Flooring. Table by Jean-Louis Deniot from Baker. Sculpture by Nour Kuri, Mexico. Heart painting by Jane Waterous from Galerie De Bellefeuille. POWDER: Sconces by Lalique. Mirror from AREA. Fixtures and Vitraform sink from Hollywood Builders Hardware. Wallcovering by Phillip Jeffries. Flooring from Pomo+ADR. LIVING ROOM: Paneling painted in Sherwin Williams Aesthetic White and finished by Segreto. Custom rug by Madison Lily. Furnishings from Neal & Co. Baker, ILIAD, and IL Pezzo Mancante. Custom pillows with fabric from Holly Hunt and Susann Eschenfelder. KITCHEN: Plugs painted to match marble by Segreto. Custom kitchen hood by James Dawson Design, Inc. Barstools from Meredith O'Donnell.

BRINGING THE OUTSIDE IN (PAGES 288–293)

Designers Mary Jane Gallagher Interior Design, Michelle Stewart Design. Renovation Architect Cusimano Architect. Renovator Kerr Construction LLC. Photographer Wade Blissard. Segreto Consultant Kirby Sinclair. FAMILY ROOM: Plaster fireplace by Segreto. Gracie Wallcovering from Ken Kehoe & Company. Custom rug by STARK. Custom sofa by Designer Services, Inc. in Perennials fabric from David Sutherland. Coffee table, pillows, swivel barrel chairs and brass andirons from Shabby Slips. Brass lamps from AREA. LIBRARY: Fireplace finish by Segreto. Art above the fireplace and white chairs from Shabby Slips. Pink sofa, pillows and coffee table from M Naeve. KITCHEN: Cabinet finishes by Segreto.

A RETREAT ON THE RAVINE (PAGES 294–299)

Designer Jennifer Rigamonti. Renovator Doyle Construction, Jim Bob Taylor. Photographer Wade Blissard. Segreto Consultants Leslie Sinclair, Kirby Sinclair. FAMILY ROOM: Finish on stone by Segreto. Reclaimed fireplace from Chateau Domingue. Furnishings from homeowner, AREA and Spaces for Home. Artwork by Jo Hyman. KITCHEN/BAR: SegretoStone® counters, plaster hood and cabinet finishes by Segreto. Counter stools from Mecox. Pendants from Brown. Reclaimed tiles behind stove from Chateau Domingue. POWDER: Venetian plaster by Segreto.

KITCHENS (PAGES 300–319)

(PAGES 302-303) Designer Lindsey Herod Interiors. Renovator Goodchild Custom Homes and Renovations, John Goodchild. Photographer Laurey Glenn. Plaster by Segreto. Segreto Consultant Leslie Sinclair. Faucet and pot filler from Waterworks. Pendant lighting from The Urban Electric Co. Sconces from Visual Comfort & Co. White vases from Joyce Horn Antiques. Low white bowl by Tina Frey Designs. Cabinet hardware from Rejuvenation. Marble countertops from Pomo+ADR.

(PAGES 304-305) Architectural Consultant Sarah West & Associates. Building Designer Rice Residential Design L.L.C. Builder Abercrombie Custom Homes, L.P. Photographer Wade Blissard. Segreto Consultant Kirby Sinclair. Plaster by Segreto. Barstools from Interlude Home. Antique tile from L'Antiquaro Antique Encaustic Tile. Barstools from Interlude Home.

(PAGE 306) Designer Nest & Cot. Photographer Wade Blissard. Segreto Consultant Leslie Simmons. Armoire, cabinet and plaster finishes by Segreto. Hood and kitchen accessories from Joyce Horn Antiques. Island top from Floor Designs of Houston. Farm table from Janet Wiebe. Concrete perimeter kitchen counters and vanity top by Spirit Ridge Studios.

(PAGE 307) Designer Maison Maison Design; Suzanne Duin. Architect and Builder Butler Brothers. Photographer TK Images. Segreto Consultants Leslie Sinclair, Andrea Condara. Plaster by Segreto. Plaster and cabinet finishes by Segreto. Kitchen hanging lights and buffet lamps from Circa Lighting with custom lampshades by Maison Maison. Plumbing fixtures from Hollywood Builders Hardware. Quartzite from Earth Stone.

(PAGES 308–309) Designer Cindy Witmer Designs. Building Designer Robert Dame Designs. Builder Stonehenge Classic Homes Inc. Photographer Laurey Glenn. Segreto Consultant Leslie Sinclair. Plaster and SegretoStone® counters by Segreto. Reclaimed wood door fronts from Custom Floors Unlimited. Light fixture from Formations. Backsplash behind range from Walker Zanger. Limestone flooring from Alkusari Stone. Beams from Woodshop of Texas. Steel doors from Portella. Breakfast chairs from Restoration hardware. Breakfast table from Thompson + Hanson Stone House.

(PAGES 310–313) Designer Stanley Ellis Inc. Architect Joshua I. F. Jones. Renovator Daniel Johnson, D.H.I. Photographer Laurey Glenn. Segreto consultants Leslie Sinclair, Andrea Condara. Cabinet finishes and painted concrete floors by Segreto. Albertine range CornuFe 90. Cabinets built by John Yaremko. Shaw sink, faucet cabinet hinges and knobs from Fixtures & Fittings. Shelves from Urban Archaeology. Mirror from Lone Star Glass, Inc.

(PAGE 314) Designer Maison Blanche Design LLC. Architect Rice Residential Design L.L.C. Builder: Bella Torre Homes. Photographer: TK Images; Tad Krampitz. Segreto Consultant Kirby Sinclair. Cabinet finishes, plaster hood and SegretoStone® island top by Segreto. Hardware and fixtures from Acero Bella. Marble countertop from ARIA Stone Gallery. Bull head from MAI Memorial Antiques & Interiors. Barstools from Restoration Hardware. Island Pendants from Circa Lighting. Wood floors by Doro's Unique Flooring.

(PAGE 315) Designer Beverly Shaeffer. Renovator Justo & Company. Photographer Wade Blissard. Segreto Consultants Leslie Sinclair, Andrea Condara. Plaster and SegretoStone® counters and island painted Sherwin Williams Network Grey and finished by Segreto. Flooring from Materials Marketing. Backsplash tile from the Cement Tile Shop. Perimeter cabinets and trim painted Benjamin Moore Seapearl.

(PAGES 316-317) Builder David James Custom Builder. Furnishings Talbot Cooley Interiors. Building Designer Robert Dame Designs. Photographer Kerry Kirk. Segreto Consultant Kirby Sinclair. Plaster hood by Segreto. Floors by Custom Floors Unlimited. Counters from Omni Surfaces. Hardware and fixtures from Acero Bella. Lighting from Circa Lighting. Steel Doors from Cedar Mill Co.

(PAGES 318-319) Designer Lucas/Eilers Design Associates L.L.P.; Sarah Eilers. Architect Natalye Appel + Associates. Builder Jefferson Christian Custom Homes, Dale Christian. Photographer Julie Soefer. Segreto Consultant Andrea Condara. Cabinet finishes by Segreto. Faucet, sink and Rocky Mountain Hardware from Hollywood Builders Hardware. Mariana Soapstone from Walker Zanger. Antique Cement Tile from Chateau Domingue. Custom Vent Hood by Lonestar Range Hood Company. Swivel Arm Counter Stools from Hyde Park Home covered in Great Plains fabric from Holly Hunt. Metro Wall Sconce from Urban Electric Co. Antique Inspired Khotan Runner from Matt Camron Rugs & Tapestries.

BATHROOMS (PAGES 320–341)

(PAGES 322–323) Designer Riley Suffel. Renovator Goodchild Custom Homes and Renovations. Photographer Wade Blissard. Segreto Consultants Leslie Sinclair, Leslie Simmons. Photograph by Lalya Salek. Concrete counters by Gunnells Concrete Inc. Rug and lighting from Round Top Texas. Stools from BROWN. Marble from Chateau Dominque.

(PAGES 324–325) Architectural Consultant Sarah West & Associates. Building Designer Rice Residential Design L.L.C. Builder Abercrombie Custom Homes, L.P. Photographer Wade Blissard. Segreto Consultant Kirby Sinclair. Raised plaster walls, SegretoStone® counters and door finish by Segreto.

(PAGES 326–327) ADJACENT IMAGE: Designer Ken Kehoe & Company. Builder Cupic Custom Homes. Photographer Wade Blissard. Segreto consultant Leslie Sinclair. Door and Cabinet finishes by Segreto. OPPOSITE IMAGE: Designer Maison Maison Design; Suzanne Duin. Architect and Builder Butler Brothers. Photographer TK Images. Segreto Consultants Leslie Sinclair, Andrea Condara. Plaster by Segreto. French Bague's chandelier and sconces from 1st Dibs. Plumbing fixtures from Hollywood Builders Hardware. Marble from Walker Zanger.

(PAGES 328–329) Designer Trisha McGaw Designs. Building Designer Robert Dame Designs. Builder Allan Edwards Builder Inc. Photographer Julie Soefer. Segreto Consultants Leslie Sinclair, Kirby Sinclair. Gold leafing on cabinetry by Segreto. Hardware from Hollywood Builders Hardware.

(PAGES 330–331) OPPOSITE IMAGE: Designer Nest & Cot. Photographer Wade Blissard. Segreto Consultant Leslie Simmons. Plaster and cabinet restoration Segreto. Sconces and sink from Chateau Dominque. Concrete vanity top by Spirit Ridge Studios. Bath accessories from Kuhl-Linscomb. ABOVE IMAGE: Designer Beverly Schaeffer. Renovator Justo & Company. Photographer Wade Blissard. Segreto Consultants Leslie Sinclair, Andrea Condara. Plaster and cabinet finishes by Segreto. Plumbing from Morrison Supply. Hardware from Acero Bella.

(PAGES 332–333) Designer Cindy Witmer Designs. Building Designer Robert Dame Designs. Builder Stonehenge Classic Homes Inc. Photographer Laurey Glenn. Segreto Consultant Leslie Sinclair. Plaster and cabinet finishes by Segreto. Tile from Redondo Tile & Stone. Fjord counters from Pomo+ADR. Hardware from Rocky Mountain Hardware. Lighting from Formations. Steel doors from Portella. Shades from The Shade Shop.

(PAGES 334–335) OPPOSITE IMAGE: Architectural Consultant and Designer Sarah West & Associates. Building Designer Robert Dame Designs. Builder Parker House, Inc. Photographer Michael Hunter. Segreto Consultant Leslie Sinclair. Limewash by Segreto. ABOVE IMAGE: Designer Elizabeth Garrett Interiors. Architect Architectural Solutions, Inc. Builder Cupic Custom Homes. Photographer Wade Blissard. Segreto Consultants Leslie Sinclair, Kirby Sinclair. Gold leaf cabinet detail by Segreto. Glass tile behind vanity from Ann Sacks.

(PAGE 336) Designer Sallie Davis. Architect Architectural Solutions, Inc. Builder D. L. Doyle Construction. Photographer Wade Blissard. Segreto Consultant Leslie Sinclair. Mural by Segreto. Hardware, fixtures and Circa Lighting scones from Hollywood Builders Hardware.

(PAGE 337) Designer Bailey Vermillion Interiors; Sheri Bailey. Architect Newberry Architecture. Builder Goodchild Custom Homes and Renovations. Photographer Wade Blissard. Segreto Consultant Leslie Sinclair. Plaster by Segreto. Soap stone from Arizona Tile fabricated by

Sweeney Marble. Rocky Mountain Hardware from Fixture and Fittings. Sconces and art from M Naeve. Mirror from Egg Collective.

(PAGES 338–339) Designer Claudia Lummis. Architect Builder Windham Builders. Mural and cabinet finishes by Segreto.

THE JOURNEY TO ALWAYS CREATE (PAGES 342–349)

Designer Shann Kastendieck. Client Valobra Master Jewelers. Photographer Wade Blissard. Segreto consultants Leslie Sinclair, Kirby Sinclair. Raised florals by Segreto.

Designer Diana Humphrey. Architect Robert Levy + Associates. Contractor Goodman Even Inc. Photographer Laurey Glenn. Segreto Consultants Leslie Sinclair, Kirby Sinclair. BED: Plaster and relief wall by Segreto. Trim color Sherwin Williams Highland White. Headboard recovered by The Joseph Company. Swaim night stands from John Brooks. Art on shelf left to right by: Lissa Hunt from Munson Gallery, Lance Letscher and Michael Still from McMurtry Gallery. BATH: Tadelakt plaster and stone sculptures by Segreto. Cabinetry from Eggersmann. Boyd sconces from Donghia. Fixtures from Westheimer Plumbing & Hardware. Counters and shower material from Houston Stone Center. Flooring from Thorntree. Mirrors from Artists' Framing Resource. Art by Michael Sell from McMurtrey Gallery.

Builder David James Custom Builder. Furnishings by Talbot Cooley. Building Designer Robert Dame Designs. Photography by Kerry Kirk. Segreto Consultant Kirby Sinclair. Coffee table from Somar Creations. Rug from Madison Lily. Club chairs from Hallman Furniture upholstered in fabric from Barrow Industries. Lumbar pillow in Creations Metaphors fabric from Kravet. Custom Sofa by The Joseph Company upholstered in Villa Romo fabric from Culp & Associates. Floor lamp from Bungalow 5. Art by Michael Von Helms from Dimmitt Contemporary Art. Rosemary Hallgarten throw from Holland & Sherry

SEGRETOSTONE® (PAGES 350–357)

Room designed by Leslie Sinclair, Kirby Sinclair. Photographer Wade Blissard. Plaster, Aidan Gray plastered over light fixture, cabinet finishes and SegretoStone® coffee table by Segreto. Rug from Madison Lily. Couch from Cantoni. Stools and pillows on couch from Lam Bespoke. Swivel chairs from John Brooks covered in velvet from High Fashion Home, with pillows from Boxwood Interiors. Two side chairs from Round Top Antiques Show upholstered by Manuel Ruiperez. Drapery linen and trim from Interior Fabrics sewn by Rosa. Tray from Mecox.

Segreto designer for SegretoStone® outdoor loungers, sink and custom door, Isai Marrder, fabricated by Segreto. Photographer Pär Bengtsson.

Designer Shannon Crain Design. Builder Riverway Development, Inc. Photographer Kerry Kirk. Segreto consultant Kirby Sinclair. SegretoStone® fireplace by Segreto. Mirrors from Round Top Antique Show. Accent tables from Jessica Lez Antiques. Custom coffee table from THE CEH. Art over mantel by Holly Addi. Furniture from Highland House. Pillow fabric by Rose Tarlow. Lamps from Visual Comfort & Co.

Designer Marie Flanigan Interiors; Marie Flanigan, Kelsey Grant. Contractor Midway. Photographers Julie Soefer, Wade Blissard. Segreto Consultant Leslie Sinclair, assistant Karly Rauch. Cash wrap finish, SegretoStone® counters and floating sinks in his and her baths by Segreto. Furnishings from Lam Bespoke. Cash wrap built by Doro's Unique Flooring. Tasmania wood flooring in Scamander colorway from Master Craft. Eugene Large Pendants from Visual Comfort.

Woman's powder Rene sconces from Visual Comfort. Mirror from Bliss. Men's powder Union Filament clear glass sconces and Gabby mirror from Restoration Hardware.

SEGRETO PAINT (PAGES 358–359)

LEFT: Photographer Pär Bengtsson. RIGHT: Designer Rachael Miclette. Renovator Morrisett Construction. Photographer Wade Blissard.

NEW USES FOR AGE-OLD MATERIALS (PAGES 360–363)

Designer Garrett Hunter. Architect Michael T. Landrum Inc. Builder Sawyer Enterprises. Photographer Wade Blissard. Segreto Consultant Leslie Sinclair. Limewash by Segreto. Reclaimed fireplace and flooring from Chateau Domingue.

Building Designer Robert Dame Designs. Builder Abercrombie Custom Homes, L.P. Photographer TK Images. Segreto Consultant Leslie Sinclair. Limewash by Segreto.

DEVELOPING A PLAN (PAGES 364–369)

Designer Leslie Strauss Interiors. Builder Bentley Custom Homes. Photographer Wade Blissard. Segreto Consultants Leslie Sinclair, Kirby Sinclair. DINING ROOM: Plaster floors and cabinet glazing by Segreto. Trim painted in Sherwin Williams Zircon. Built-ins painted Sherwin Williams March Wind and glazed by Segreto. Furniture and chandeliers from Ladco Design Center. KITCHEN: Cabinets painted Sherwin Williams March Wind and glazed by Segreto. Walls and trim painted Benjamin Moore Decorator's White. Decorative tile from Designer Floors of Houston. FAMILY ROOM: Built-ins painted Sherwin Williams Peppercorn glazed by Segreto. Furniture from Ladco Design Center. Walls and trim painted Benjamin Moore Decorator's White. Light fixtures from Lighting Inc. POWDER ROOM: Cabinet finishes by Segreto. Wall covering from Philip Jeffries. Sconces from Visual Comfort. Mirror from Ladco Design Center.

RECONFIGURING SPACES (PAGES 370–375)

Renovation Architect Newberry Architecture; Clint Johnson. Builder Parker House Inc. Photographer Wade Blissard. Plaster throughout by Segreto. Segreto Consultant Leslie Sinclair. KITCHEN: Slurried brick and SegretoStone® counters by Segreto. Metal hood by ACI Metal Works. Antique fireback from Chateau Domingue. Concrete pendant from Brown. Metal bakers' rack from Rocky Mountain Hardware. Appliances from K&N Sales. LIVING ROOM: Chandelier from Made Goods. Rug from Rug Mart Houston. Chairs and couch by Creative Style Furniture. Coffee table from Restoration Hardware. PANTRY/HER OFFICE: SegretoStone® counters by Segreto. Iron door by ACI Metal Works. Hardware by Ashley Norton. Reclaimed concrete tiles from Chateau Domingue.

CREATING IMPACT (PAGES 376–377)

Photographer Wade Blissard. Segreto Consultants Leslie Sinclair, Kirby Sinclair. Silver Leaf, graphic on floors and stenciled walls by Segreto.

PLASTERS (PAGES 378–379)

LEFT: Techniques by Segreto. RIGHT: Designer Cindy Witmer Designs. Building Designer Robert Dame Designs. Builder Stonehendge Classic Homes Inc. Photographer Laurey Glenn. Segreto Consultant Leslie Sinclair. Plaster and cabinet finishes by Segreto. Reclaimed wood flooring by Custom Floors Unlimited.

DECORATIVE PAINTING (PAGES 380–383)

LEFT: Designer Trisha McGaw Designs. Renovator Pinnacle Custom Builders. Photographer Wade Blissard. Segreto Consultants Leslie Sinclair, Kirby Sinclair. Plaster, stenciling and SegretoStone® floating vanity by Segreto. White onyx sink from Ferguson. OC-Devotion Offset Gilt backsplash from Materials Marketing. Gas lanterns by Carolina Lanterns. Planters from Restoration Hardware. RIGHT: Techniques by Segreto.

Stencil over limestone, Designer Jennifer Martinez. Builder Fairway Companies. Fireplace with panel surround, Designer Nest & Cot. Photographer on all Wade Blissard. Segreto Consultants Leslie Sinclair, Leslie Simmons. Decorative finishes by Segreto.

WOOD (PAGES 384–385)

LEFT: Designer Claudia Lummis. Builder Windham Builders. Photographer Wade Blissard. Segreto Consultant Leslie Sinclair. Gold leafing, staircase finish and glazing by Segreto. RIGHT: Techniques by Segreto.

MURALS (PAGES 386–387)

LEFT: Murals by Segreto. RIGHT: Designed by Leslie Sinclair, Kirby Sinclair. Photographer Wade Blissard. Mural, paneling finish and SegretoStone® coffee table by Segreto. Settee from Joyce Horn Antiques coved in John Saladino mohair from Ken Kehoe & Company.

MY FAVORITE GAME OF I SPY (PAGES 388–389)

Designer Triangle Interiors. Builder Goodchild Custom Homes and Renovations. Photographer Michael Hunter. Segreto Consultant Leslie Sinclair. Vents and cans by Segreto.

SOURCES (PAGES 390–403)

Designer Shannon Crain Design. Builder Riverway Development, Inc. Photographer Kerry Kirk. Segreto Consultant Kirby Sinclair. Plaster and mural by Segreto. Credenza from CEH. Lighting from Visual Comfort.

Designer Triangle Interiors. Photographer Kerry Kirk. Waxed plaster by Segreto. Artwork by Sara Glenn from Dimmitt Contemporary Art. Chandelier from Currey and Company. Chair Fabric from Clarence House. Rug from Turkish Carpets, Inc. Floor Lamp from Circa Lighting. Drapery fabric from Schumacher bordered in Houles Trim. Segreto Consultant Kirby Sinclair.

Library of Congress Cataloging-in-Publication Data
NAMES: Sinclair, Leslie
TITLE: Segreto Impressions / Leslie Sinclair.
DESCRIPTION: First Edition.

ISBN: 978-1-61850-153-0

Self-Published by Segreto.

GRAPHIC DESIGN: Limb Design—Houston, Texas
COPY EDITOR: Caitlin Tunney
PRINTER: Four Colour

Printed and bound in The United States of America

To order additional copies or for more information
www.segretofinishes.com

Segreto Finishes
414 Antoine
Houston, TX 77055
713.461.5210

leslie@segretofinishes.com

In the making of this book, every attempt has been made to verify names and facts.
We apologize if any errors have been made.

LIMITED FIRST EDITION